Published by Ockley Books Limited

First published December 2017, Revised edition published November 2020

Front cover photos supplied by Offside Sports Photography Ltd
and UK Sports Pics.

Foreword written by and copyright of Geoffrey Boycott

ISBN 978-1-910906-21-7

Layout & design by Michael Kinlan,
edited by David Hartrick and Roger Domeneghetti

Printed & bound by:
Biddles Printing, King's Lynn

DAVID COOKE

WAS GRACE BETTER THAN BRADMAN?

A NEW WAY TO RANK ASHES CRICKETERS

OCKLEY BOOKS
.com

This is the first book by David Cooke. A retired
Chartered Accountant and lifelong cricket fan, he is
married with three sons and lives in Buckinghamshire.

To my wife Helga and sons Chris, Sam and George,
for their advice and encouragement throughout.

CONTENTS

PREFACE	IX
FOREWORD BY SIR GEOFFREY BOYCOTT	XIII
HOW SHOULD WE COMPARE PLAYERS?	17
1877 TO 1912	25
1920 TO 1938	43
1946 TO THE 1977 CENTENARY TEST	57
1977 TO 2000	73
2001 TO 2019	87
THE CURRENT PLAYERS	103
PLAYERS WHO JUST MISSED THE CUT	111
THE ALL-ROUNDERS	119
THE WICKETKEEPERS	133
THE CAPTAINS	141
REVIEW OF RESULTS	175
BEYOND AVERAGES	181
ALL-TIME TEAMS FOR ENGLAND AND AUSTRALIA	187
APPENDIX	219

PREFACE

The origin of this book was in conversations with my father-in-law Steve Houghton (no mean cricketer himself - he captained Singapore for two periods in the 1960s and early 70s) in which we discussed the difficulties in making comparisons of sporting greats across the ages. For cricket I felt that batting and bowling averages needed some adjustments to make them more suitable for comparing players who had played in widely different conditions many years apart. The method I evolved to do this is explained in Chapter 1 and the adjusted averages produced by the method are at the heart of the book.

As well as enabling new numerical comparisons to be made the adjusted averages have given me a backdrop against which to trace the history of the Ashes and discuss the many changes in playing conditions and laws of the game that have taken place over the years.

In addition to the batting and bowling comparisons I have added sections on wicketkeepers, all-rounders and captains using different comparison methods. I much enjoyed writing all of this, not least the final chapters on my own best teams for England and Australia.

I have consulted a number of books and sources in carrying out the necessary research and the principal ones are listed below. I should mention several books especially. "The Wisden Book of Test Cricket" which gives the full scorecards of all Test matches played was the main source of raw data and "Wisden on the Ashes" and the annual Wisden almanacs were also very useful.

To put my own rankings and my own choice of an all-time England XI and an all-time Australian XI in context, I used, and have quoted widely from, three books: "The Best XI" by Geoffrey

Boycott, "Bradman's Best Ashes Teams" by Roland Perry and "The Top 100 Cricketers Of All Time" by Christopher Martin-Jenkins. Malcolm Knox's excellent book "The Captains" provided a great insight into the Australian Ashes captains and the way the role has evolved over the years.

The main books consulted were:

The Wisden Book of Test Cricket 1877-1984
The Wisden Book of Test Cricket 1977-2000
The Wisden Book of Test Cricket 2000-2009
Wisden on the Ashes
The Best XI - Geoffrey Boycott
Bradman's Best Ashes Teams - Roland Perry
The Top 100 Cricketers Of All Time - Christopher Martin-Jenkins
The Captains - Malcolm Knox
England v Australia - David Frith
Double Century - Tony Lewis
Beyond a Boundary - C L R James
Who's Who of test cricketers - Christopher Martin-Jenkins
W G Grace - Simon Rae
The First Test Match – Stanley Brogden & John Arlott
Cricket: The Great Ones – John Arlott
The Changing Face of Cricket - A G Moyes
S F Barnes, Master Bowler - Leslie Duckworth
Ten Great Innings - Ralph Barker
Archie – A biography of A C MacLaren - Michael Down
In Quest of the Ashes - Douglas Jardine
Walter Hammond - Gerald Howat
The Great Bowlers - John Arlott
The Great Captains - A A Thomson
Hutton & Washbrook - A A Thomson
Giants of the Game - RH Lyttleton, WJ Ford, CB Fry and G Giffen
Beyond Ten thousand - Allan Border
Ashes to Ashes - Peter Roebuck
Ashes 97 - Norman Geras & Ian Holliday
Jack Hobbs - John Arlott
Elusive Victory - EW Swanton

I must also thank my publisher Dave Hartrick of Ockley Books for his faith in the book and his hard work in bringing it to publication. Designer Mick Kinlan and editor Roger Domeneghetti have also played key roles.

This second edition has been updated for the Ashes series in Australia in 2017/18 and in England in 2019. In addition, the method for calculating the bowling averages, described in Chapter 1, has been refined and it has been possible to use more sophisticated data processing techniques resulting in some corrections to the original manually extracted data. I must thank my brother Patrick Cooke for his advice and assistance in these updates and revisions for the second edition.

David Cooke
October 2019

FOREWORD BY SIR GEOFFREY BOYCOTT

As I've said before, statistics don't lie but nor do they tell the whole story. Great players will have great figures but comparing players across the ages is difficult. I know this because I've made these comparisons myself in my own book "The Best XI".

David's book proposes a method to adjust averages to allow better player comparison across the ages. By limiting the book to England v Australia Test matches only, the comparisons are more accurate and have been integrated into the story of the Ashes Tests from their beginnings in 1877 (in fact they weren't called the Ashes until after 1882). The story is told through the different eras and from the viewpoints of the batsmen, bowlers, all-rounders, wicketkeepers and captains.

Let me remind you how big the changes across the years have been. (Much of this is taken directly from my own book but I make no apology for that because I can't say it better than I did there).

In the early years the pitches were poor with stones on them for heaven's sake, and even when they improved they were still open to the elements so batting was much more difficult; as the number of low scoring games proves, bowlers controlled situations and dominated.

Then we have to look at the leg-before law which prior to 1935 dictated that the ball had to pitch in line from wicket to wicket and be going on to hit the stumps. So automatically batsmen went back and across which negated a lot of offspin, the nip-back seamers and the inswinger. The law was changed on an experimental basis in 1935 and the change became permanent in 1937.

Fast bowlers were pretty toothless up until the bodyline tour of 1932-33 because they were expected to pitch it up outside or on off stump. It was just not the done thing to bowl at a batsman's ribs – "not cricket" as the Aussies whinged. There was no systematic attempt to intimidate or put the batsmen under pressure by making them think they were going to get hurt. All that was to change.

It was not until much later that covering of pitches became standard. In Australia uncovered pitches normally didn't matter too much because they didn't get a lot of rain, but when it did come down you ended up with a "sticky dog" and the pitch was unplayable. That didn't change until 1954-55 when full covering was introduced at the start of Len Hutton's tour, but in England it didn't happen until 1979. The Test and County Cricket Board (forerunner of the England and Wales Cricket Board, ECB) said: "At the behest of overseas bowlers and in fairness to the paying public, pitches for Test matches in England will be fully covered at all times". Thank you very much. I had 15 years on uncovered pitches and some of them were very juicy, let me tell you. In my first Test at Trent Bridge against Australia in 1964 I was 23 not out overnight when it rained and next morning Garth McKenzie broke my finger. That's the difference between uncovered and covered pitches.

There's a difference in equipment too. No helmets, not even batting gloves in WG's day and when they were introduced they were only flimsy cotton affairs with little rubber spikes on the back right up until the 1940s when the horsehair glove came in. Bats are now heavier and better and hit the ball harder and further and have evolved like golf clubs and tennis racquets. Even the wickets increased in size to 28 in tall by 9 in wide in 1931. In 1969, the experimental change which began in 1963 was made permanent and the no-ball law changed in all Test cricket from a bowler being required to keep his *back* foot behind the return crease to keeping his *front* foot behind the popping crease (the front line where the batsman stands). Sir Donald Bradman said the alteration was "the worst thing that has happened to cricket" and other illustrious commentators like Richie Benaud agree. So do I.

Overarm bowling wasn't legalised until 1864 although it was still permitted to bowl underarm and roundarm. By the time of the first official Test bowling as we know it today was standard although WG stuck to roundarm for a while. We've also had four-ball, six-ball and eight ball overs round the world at various times and one ball for the whole of an innings, however long. Bradman's 1948 team in England were allowed a new ball at 55 overs; I wouldn't have fancied facing Lindwall, Miller and big Bill Johnston with a new cherry that often. There were also timeless Tests which meant that batsmen were never under pressure to score quickly.

All these changes over the years have a bearing on the runs scored and wickets taken in all Test matches. So – yes, figures are a vital part of the assessment but I think you have to study them and it's how we interpret them that's important.

The adjusted average method in the book interprets the conventional statistics in a way that caters for all these changes and more besides. The player rankings have got one or two surprises in them which is always good for a debate!

HOW SHOULD WE COMPARE PLAYERS?

It is now more than 140 years since the first ever Test match was played, between England and Australia. Twelve years later South Africa made their first Test appearance. The West Indies made theirs in 1928, followed by New Zealand in 1930, India in 1932, Pakistan in 1952, Sri Lanka in 1982, Zimbabwe in 1992, Bangladesh in 2000 and both Afghanistan and Ireland in 2018.

More than 2,500 cricketers have played at least one Test and it's natural for us to want to compare them. Although cricket is a team game, the way it's played means that individual performances are measured directly in assessing the result. Because of that not only do we want to know the teams' scores but also the runs scored by each batsman and the wickets taken by each bowler. The outcome is a much greater proliferation of data on individual performances than in, say, rugby or football, where it is only comparatively recently that data beyond merely the number of games played and the number of tries or goals scored has been captured.

With all this cricket data there quickly grew up widely accepted methods for comparing players. For batsmen popular measures were total runs, highest score, average score and number of centuries. For bowlers, total wickets taken, average runs conceded for each wicket and most wickets in a match were considered important. Because most other measures are dependent on the number of matches played, it seems generally accepted that to the extent a player can be measured by numbers, the average runs per dismissal for a batsman and the average runs per wicket conceded by a bowler are the most important figures.

I emphasise "...to the extent a player can be measured by numbers...". Surely the most interesting discussions about the merits of players do not involve numbers at all but instead consider subjective opinions about who is the greatest leader, can bowl the fastest, or has the most beautiful cover drive. Nevertheless averages are here to stay.

This book starts by suggesting a method of adjusting averages in order to mitigate some of their limitations. Then I review the figures for these adjusted averages for the top players through history based on Test matches between England and Australia.

This approach might prompt some questions for example:

What are these limitations in averages?

How can the normal averages, (I call them "raw" averages) be adjusted?

Why look only at matches between England and Australia?

LIMITATIONS IN AVERAGES

Raw averages take no account of playing conditions. A half century on a difficult pitch against tough opposition is treated in exactly the same way as one in easy conditions. Many matters affect the overall playing conditions and the balance between batsman and bowler, and the combined effect can be enormous, particularly when comparing early Test matches with those in the inter-war years or in more recent times. For example, few of us would attempt to use averages to compare Clem Hill, one of the leading early Australian batsmen with Michael Clarke. Our acceptance that we can't really use averages for that purpose, and the fact that it is unlikely that there is anyone who will have seen both Hill and Clarke play, probably means we don't make much, if any, attempt to make such comparisons between players from these different eras. Except that we effectively do just that when we select our greatest ever England, Australian or even combined XI. In that case the raw averages just aren't suitable. There is virtually no batsman in early Ashes cricket who has an average over 40 and many early Ashes bowlers have better averages than even the most revered of their later compatriots. Yet, few would suggest that a Greatest Ever XI should be composed only of bowlers from the early Ashes tests and batsmen from later ones. The reality is that the balance between batsman and bowler has changed considerably over the years due to a number of factors including developments in pitch preparation and changes in the LBW and no ball laws. These factors can affect the raw averages significantly.

HOW CAN RAW AVERAGES BE ADJUSTED?

Any attempt to adjust averages for particular factors like pitch conditions, rule changes, quality of the opposition would be subjective and arbitrary. However there is an automatic, objective measure of the impact of these and other factors. All of them affect the overall average runs scored per wicket taken in a given match. So, a 50 scored in a match where the average runs per wicket is only 20 should count for more than a 50 in a match where the average runs per wicket is 30.

A calculation of the average runs scored (excluding extras) per wicket in all Test matches between England and Australia, from the first Test, in Melbourne in 1877, to the last at the time of writing, at Sydney in 2018, gives a figure of approximately 28.9.

The standard method of calculating a batsman's average of course is to divide his total runs scored by the number of times he has been dismissed. The method used in this book for calculating a batsman's "adjusted average" involves adjusting the total aggregate of runs scored before dividing by the number of dismissals. The adjustment is made on a match-by-match basis for each batsman by scaling the runs he has scored up or down according to whether the average runs per wicket scored in that match is, respectively, below or above the overall average of 28.9. A similar exercise is carried out for bowlers by adjusting the runs conceded in each match.

As an example, consider a low scoring match in the early history of the Ashes where the average runs per wicket was 14.45—just half of the overall average of 28.9 mentioned above. A batting score of 50 in this match would be scaled up by a factor of two (28.9 divided by 14.45) and so taken as a score of 100. All scores for an individual batsman are adjusted, aggregated and then divided by the total number of times the batsman has been dismissed.

For bowlers the principle is the same though the calculation is slightly different. The number of runs conceded by each bowler is adjusted on a match-by-match basis, aggregated and then divided by the total number of wickets the bowler has taken. The match-by-match adjustment is made by scaling up or down the number of runs according to whether the average runs conceded by the bowlers in that match is, respectively below or above the overall average of runs conceded per wicket taken in England v Australia Tests overall.

The difference in the calculation for bowlers arises because runs conceded by bowlers are not quite the same as runs scored by batsmen. Following a rule change in the 1980s which was effective for the 1985 Ashes series onwards, wides and no balls have been counted as runs conceded by the bowler. In addition wickets taken by the bowlers differ from total wickets that have fallen because run outs are ignored. On this basis the overall average of runs conceded per wicket taken by bowlers over all England v Australia Tests to date is 30.1. So in a match where the bowling average per wicket was 15.05 (half the overall bowling average of 30.1) a bowler who conceded 50 runs would have those runs scaled up to 100, aggregated with his other adjusted figures, in the same way as for batsmen, and then divided, by the total number of wickets he has taken.

In broad overview, batsmen and bowlers who have played predominantly in low scoring matches will have their averages adjusted upwards and those who have played predominantly in high scoring matches will have their averages adjusted downwards.

We can then rank the players both according to their "raw" averages and their "adjusted" averages, explore the changes and discuss both the merits of the adjusted averages and what they tell us about the players from different eras.

WHY ONLY LOOK AT MATCHES BETWEEN ENGLAND AND AUSTRALIA?

The average runs per wicket in any match is affected by the batting (and bowling) performances of both sides. If one side is much superior to the other, players on that superior side will tend to enjoy better results compared with their results against stronger sides. When comparing players, those who have played more games against weaker opposition will be advantaged.

If we look just at matches between England and Australia this advantage is eliminated. We still need the adjustment mechanism of course to take account of the changing conditions between the ages as discussed above.

GENERAL

A book purely on how to adjust averages would not be very exciting. To give the numbers some context and to review the factors which have caused variations in the batting/bowling balance I have attempted a brief review of the history of the matches which have been played between England and Australia and also a brief look at the careers of the key players.

To do this I have divided the history into five eras as follows:

1. 1877-1912
The first England-Australia Test to the
last pre-First World War Ashes series

2. 1921-1938
Including all the inter-war Ashes series

3. 1946-1977
The first post-War Ashes series to the Centenary Test match

4. 1977-1999
The first Ashes series following the Centenary Test
until the end of the 20th Century

5. 2001-2019
All 21st century Ashes series up to the most recent
series in England

PLAYERS FEATURED

All batsmen who have scored at least 1,500 runs and all bowlers who have taken at least 75 wickets have been included. To these I have made just one addition and that is WG Grace. He scored just 1,098 runs but because he was nearly 30 when the first Test match was played, and was able to go on only one tour to Australia in which Tests were played, he was only able to play in 22 matches despite playing Ashes Tests until he was more than 50 years old (which made him the oldest player to have represented England against Australia). The only batsmen who had played fewer completed innings than WG at the end of their Ashes careers and yet managed to reach the 1,500 runs qualification were batsmen in eras where raw averages were much higher because the batting/bowling balance had swung towards batsmen.

The reality is that WG had little real opportunity of achieving the qualification requirements and moreover it would not make sense to write a book aimed at comparing players across the ages and leave him out. However, he is the only exception. In all other cases it is only those meeting the criteria who have been included in the core players (61 batsmen and 43 bowlers) whose figures have been analysed to produce adjusted averages and adjusted rankings. There are a few players who have narrowly failed to make the conditions or are of interest because of their particular fame and they are discussed in Chapter 8. In addition, the top current players are considered in Chapter 7.

All this is about batsmen and bowlers, but all-rounders and wicket keepers are of interest too and they are covered in Chapters 9 and 10. There are four all-rounders who meet both the batting and bowling conditions and an additional two who have scored 1,000 runs and taken 50 wickets are also included. To those six core all-rounders I have added some more who fall a little short of the condition of 1,000 runs and 50 wickets but are of particular interest.

Wicket keepers must have 50 dismissals to qualify.

DEFINITIONS OF TERMS

It is convenient to define certain terms, representing some of the concepts in the book, that are not universal cricket terms:

"RAW AVERAGE"

this is the average as calculated according to the normal cricket convention

"ADJUSTED AVERAGE"

this is the average for a player calculated as above to take account of the average runs per wicket in the games in which he scored runs as a batsman or in which he conceded runs as a bowler.

"SUCCESS PERCENTAGE"

this is a measure of the success of the team in the matches played by a particular individual. One point is awarded for each game won, half a point for each game drawn, and no points for games lost. These points are added together and then divided by the number of games.

(In this book I sometimes refer to the strike rate of wickets per match for bowlers but do not refer to the strike rate of balls per wicket, which is of course much more commonly used today. This is because the balls per wicket measure is very dependent on the prevailing conditions whereas wickets per match is not so dependent, there always having been a maximum of 20 wickets available to be taken).

1877 TO 1912

This first era covers the period from the first Test match between England and Australia in 1877 up to 1912 which was the last series played before World War 1. Ninety four of the 356 games between England and Australia up to the end of the 2019 series were played during this era. The careers of 10 of the 61 batsmen and 12 of the 43 bowlers featured in this book occurred primarily in this era.

In the early decades, little of the structure we take for granted today was present. For example, it wasn't until England's tour of Australia in the winter of 1897/98 that it became normal for a series to consist of five matches, and it was also around this time that the teams began to be reasonably representative of the best of each country.

Tours to Australia started in the 1860s and were initially unofficial ventures organised between Australian clubs and private promoters in England. WG Grace himself took a team to Australia in the winter of 1873/74. While none of the 15 games were considered first class, it was the first English tour Down Under for a decade providing the game with a much-needed boost in Australia. On these early tours the English teams were considered superior and regularly played against teams with more players. Grace's team, for example, took to the pitch against a Victoria team featuring 18 players. However, on 15 March 1877 at Melbourne, James Lillywhite's English side faced Dave Gregory's Australian side on equal terms and that game subsequently became recognised as the first official Test match between the two countries. Not that this first match had fully representative sides. James Lillywhite's touring team was a financial venture arranged and sponsored by Lillywhite, Alfred Shaw and Arthur Shrewsbury. While it contained the cream of English professional players, no amateurs, such as WG Grace, took part in the tour. The Australian side consisted of players from Victoria and New South Wales.

In that late-Victorian period, the laws of the game were very different from the ones we would recognise today. Overs contained just four balls, bowlers could bowl two overs consecutively, the ball needed to pitch in line with the wickets for an LBW dismissal and the wickets and playing area could be of such poor quality that the rules catered for lost balls *within* the field of play. Sometimes the wickets were pitched east to west so that, in the words of Tom Garrett one of the Australian players in that first Test match: "at one end the sun was in your eyes and on the other end you were playing a ball out of the shadow of your own figure".

Australia won that historic first Test by 45 runs thanks largely to an innings of 165 by Charles Bannerman (who had been born in Kent) which only ended when he retired hurt with a split finger. No other Australian batsman reached 20 in that first innings and Bannerman's score remained the highest individual score in an England-Australia match until 1884. England turned the tables a little over a fortnight later, winning a second game by four wickets. The next Test was played, again at Melbourne, in January 1879 and was won by Australia by ten wickets.

It was not until 1880 that the first Test in England was played, at the Oval, with WG Grace appearing for the first time. He scored 152 out of an England score of 420 (the highest innings total at the time) to see England through to a five-wicket victory despite an innings of 153 not out from Billy Murdoch for Australia. Two years later, Australia returned to the Oval and snatched victory by just 7 runs. It was their first victory on English soil and led *The Sporting Times* to publish its famous obituary of English cricket finishing with the line: "The body will be cremated and the ashes taken to Australia".

The Ashes properly came into being after Ivo Bligh's England touring side won the deciding third game of the 1882/83 series in Australia.[1] On leaving England, Bligh had promised to "bring back the ashes of English cricket" and following the English victory some Melbourne ladies, including Florence Morphy who subsequently

---

[1] *fourth match was won by Australia but had been added later and was not considered part of the main series. It is accepted however as a Test match and is included in the overall statistics..*

became Bligh's wife, burnt a bail, sealed the ashes inside an urn and presented the urn to Bligh. Following his death in 1927 the urn was donated to Lord's where it remains in the MCC museum as a symbol of the "Ashes". Back on home soil in 1884, England won a three-Test series 1-0 thanks to victory in the second match - the first Test to be played at Lord's. A flourishing last wicket partnership in the Australian first innings was brought to an end when Billy Murdoch, the Australian captain, amazingly fielding for England as substitute for WG Grace, took a catch to dismiss Henry 'Tup' Scott for 75.

The first five-match series followed four months later in Australia and this was won 3-2 by England. Incidents continued to arise which, today, would be considered unusual in anything other than low-level club cricket. The continuing practice of players acting as substitute fielders for the opposition is a good example. In the fifth Test, which England won by an innings and 98 runs to take the series 3-2, Aussie Affie Jarvis took a catch to dismiss his teammate Fred Spofforth for the penultimate wicket.

Another example from that final match occurred when England made an objection about one of the umpires, Tom Garrett (the same player who spoke of the difficulties the sun caused on East-West wickets), and he was simply replaced by one of the Australian players. It seems umpires were drawn from the current playing body much more so than today and movements could be in either direction. One of the umpires in the fourth Test, PG McShane, made his playing debut for Australia in the fifth Test at Melbourne.

England completed the first Ashes whitewash in 1886, winning the three-match series in England thanks to the bowling of Dick Barlow, George Lohmann and Johnny Briggs and also innings of 164 at Lord's by Arthur Shrewsbury and 170 at the Oval by W.G. Grace. The first match of the next series at Sydney in 1886/87 was notable for England's lowest ever test score of 45 when they were put in to bat on a pitch that had been used for another game which had only finished the same morning. However, England rallied with both bat and ball and eventually won by 13 runs before winning the second match of that series by 71 runs.

As England and Australia were the only Test-playing nations at the time, there were more frequent Ashes series than today, but with fewer games in each. So England made the journey Down Under again the following winter, winning the only Test of the series. The Australians made the opposite journey in 1888, but were unable to break England's strangle-hold on The Ashes in what was, due to rain-affected pitches, a very low scoring series which England won 2-1. In 1890 England won another low-scoring series, this time of two matches, 2-0 with Frederick Martin taking 12 wickets at the Oval in the only Ashes Test, and one of only two Tests, that he played.

The England tour to Australia in 1891/92 was notable for two reasons. Firstly, it was WG Grace's only Test tour to Australia, and secondly, Australia won the series, by a 2-1 margin, for the first time since their triumph in England in 1882. England were back on top with a 1-0 series win in 1893. Grace put his medical skill to use in the final Test, putting Charlie Turner's dislocated finger back into place thus enabling the Australian to continue a match-saving innings of 27 and last-wicket partnership of 36 with Jack Blackham. The five-match series in Australia in 1894/95 went to the last match with England making the 296 second-innings target with six wickets in hand and they won again, by two matches to one, in England in 1896. However, Australia won by 4-1 in 1897/98 to regain the Ashes at the start of a four-series winning streak. They won the five-match series in England in 1899 1-0, before a convincing 4-1 series victory Down Under in 1901/02. The Aussies won again in England in 1902. Their 2-1 series win contained two of the closest Ashes finishes ever: Australia winning the fourth Test at Old Trafford by 3 runs and England winning the last Test at the Oval by one wicket.

England regained the Ashes with a 4-1 win in Australia in 1903/04. The series was memorable for a number of achievements. Australia's Victor Trumper was the series leading batsman with a series aggregate of 574 runs which included two centuries, most notably his 185 not out at Sydney. However, that wasn't even the highest score of the game, let alone the series. It was eclipsed by 'Tip' Foster, whose 287 for England was the highest score in Test cricket at the time[2]. The

---

[2] *Foster's record was broken by his compatriot Andy Sandham, who scored 325—the first Test triple hundred—against the West Indies in April 1930. That record stood for barely three months before Donald Bradman scored 334 against England at Headingley, also surpassing Foster's Ashes record.*

batsmen didn't have it all their own way with Wilfred Rhodes in particular causing problems for the Australians, especially with his 15 for 124 at Melbourne.

In 1905 FS Jackson won the toss in all five Tests and led England to a 2-0 series win, but Australia regained the Ashes with a 4-1 win in 1907/08 and retained them by 2-1 in England in 1909. England won the Ashes back in Australia in 1911/12 thanks to 34 wickets from Sydney Barnes and 659 runs from Jack Hobbs and they retained them in the three-match series in England a few months later, Frank Woolley taking ten wickets in the only match to achieve a result. While that 1912 Ashes series was shorter than the now-standard five matches, it was part of a triangular tournament that saw the three countries then playing test cricket (England, Australia and South Africa) each playing the other three times.[3] By now some of the old rules had gone. In 1900 the length of the over had been increased to six balls and, in 1910 a rule change directed that six runs would be awarded if the ball cleared the boundary; previously it had been only five unless the ball was hit clean out of the ground.

At the end of this first era in 1912, 94 Tests had been played with England winning 40, Australia 35 and 19 being drawn. The average batting runs per wicket during this era was 23.3, compared with the average of 28.9 for all England-Australia Tests. However, there were some large variations between the averages of individual Tests with some, particularly at the beginning of the era, being notable for very low scores.

Given the low scores during this era, all the ten batsmen who meet the qualification criteria receive a boost to their raw average and move up a few places in the adjusted rankings. Interestingly, with one exception, no average is boosted to higher than 40 and the highest position in the adjusted rankings is that of Clem Hill at a fairly lowly 26th. That exception is WG Grace who starts with a raw average of 32.29 and a ranking of 53 and moves up to an adjusted average of 50.66 and a ranking of ninth. This is by far the biggest movement for any batsman in any of the eras.

---

[3]   England were the winners, thanks to four wins in their six games. However, the tournament was not considered a success and there would not be another multi-country Test tournament until the Asian Test Championship in 1998.

Two questions arise here. First, what is it that gives WG Grace such a large adjustment? Second, why are the adjusted averages for this era generally so low?

The first question is the easier to answer as it is simply a case of how the system works. The matches in which WG Grace played were at the very beginning of Test match history and had some of the lowest scores ever seen. It is notable that WG's dominance over the other batsmen of his era is much greater than the dominance of the leading batsman in any of third, fourth and fifth eras. If only the batsmen who meet our qualification criteria are considered, Grace's dominance is comparable with Donald Bradman's dominance of the second era. This, of course, begs the question posed by the title of the book (which is discussed in more detail in Chapter 12): Was Grace better than Bradman? However, if Grace's near-contemporaries Arthur Shrewsbury and Stanley Jackson (who miss the cut, but are discussed in Chapter 8) are included, their adjusted averages are similar to WG's. Remember though that WG's prime was in the early 1870s before Test cricket started and that he played only three of his 22 tests before his 36th birthday.

The second question is much more difficult to answer. Given that the adjustment method takes into account the variation in runs per wicket between matches (that's exactly what it is set up to do), why are all the qualifying batsmen from this era other than WG at position 26 or lower?

It seems to be the case that the "specialist" batsmen of the first era outscored the other players in their teams by a lesser margin than specialist batsmen have in later eras and it is interesting to speculate as to why this might be. I'd suggest two main reasons. First, there was the quality of the pitches which was not good during this early period of Test history and would have made batting much more of a lottery. Secondly, batting was a less well-developed art; there were far fewer coaching manuals. Therefore it would not have been as easy for a dedicated batsman to develop significant superiority over the rest of the team through practice. However, the abilities of a genuinely gifted player would shine through without lesser players being easily able to reduce the gap through coaching and hard practice.

Before moving on to the figures for the main batsmen in this first era, it's worth looking at WG Grace, whose role in cricket in the last few decades of the 19th century was unique. Born near Bristol in July 1848 William Gilbert was the eighth of nine siblings, five boys and four girls. His father Henry Grace was the local GP. When WG was two the family moved to a house with an orchard which Henry cleared to create a cricket pitch that was used by the whole family on a regular basis. Throughout WG's childhood a cricket bat was never far from his hand and the development of his cricket skills was also helped enormously by his uncle, Alfred Pocock, who is credited with teaching him to play with a straight bat.

Officially an amateur player, because of his profession as a doctor (his medical qualification in 1879 was delayed a number of years by his many cricketing commitments and accomplishments in the 1870s) Grace is widely considered to have strained the MCC doctrine that, "a gentleman ought not to make any profit from playing cricket". His family were not wealthy and financial pressure was certainly present after the death of Henry Grace in 1871.

He was certainly outside the "establishment" and despite his status within the game he was not invited to captain England until his 10th test when he was already 40 years of age. Yet his prowess at cricket, which coincided with the time that cricket was being embraced by Victorian England, was such that the West Indian historian and cricket writer CLR James wrote, "Through WG Grace, cricket, the most complete expression of popular life in pre-industrial England, was incorporated into the life of the nation". James's English contemporary AA Thomson wrote that Grace was, "...not only a great Victorian; he was almost THE great Victorian for, apart from Mr Gladstone and the Queen herself, nobody was better known or more easily recognised."

WG's impact on the game is hard to overstate. Before him batsmen were either front foot or back foot players. He evolved batting technique to deal with each ball on its merits and was the first player to be recognised as competent off both front foot and back foot. Writing in 1897 Grace's teammate Ranjitsinhji said of him, "The theory of modern batting is in all its essentials the result of WG's thinking and working on the game".

In 1866 at age 18 Grace made 224 not out at the Oval, the ground record at the time, and was then given leave to compete in the 440 yards hurdles at the National Olympian games held at Crystal Palace, an event which he won.[4]

In 1871 he amassed 2,739 runs during the first class season, in the process becoming the first batsman to score more than 2,000 in a season. He repeated this in 1873 when he also took 100 wickets to become the first person to complete the "double" of 1,000 runs and 100 wickets (albeit having scored an extra 1,000 runs!).

In 1876 he made 2,000 runs for the third time, did the double for the fourth time and in one remarkable eight-day period scored 839 runs including two triple centuries, being dismissed only twice.

During his first-class career which spanned 44 seasons and ended in 1908, Grace scored nearly 55,000 runs, made 126 centuries, and took more than 2,800 wickets. Only four players in history have scored more runs and only five have taken more wickets.

Grace's test debut was in 1880 in the first Test played in England (the fourth Test played between England and Australia). WG scored 152 to help the home side to a total of 420 and victory by five wickets. This stood as the highest individual score for England until Shrewsbury's 164 in 1886 which WG promptly surpassed with 170 in the very next Test. Having secured his medical qualification in 1879 and needing to build his doctor's practice he was able to devote less time to cricket during the 1880s. There were tours to Australia in 1881/82, 1882/83, 1884/85, 1886/87 and 1887/88 none of which he felt able to participate in and it was not until 1891/92 that he took part in a Test series in Australia. He then missed the tours in 1894/95 and 1897/98 before playing his final test in 1899 in England.

The low average scores in the early games and perhaps also the fact that he was past his prime when his Test career began have contributed to his low overall raw average of 32.29 and a low raw ranking of 53rd. His adjusted average however is boosted to 50.66, and his ranking to ninth overall, the greatest improvement of any player, giving him mathematical recognition to match his universal critical acclaim.

---

[4]   *The modern Olympic games began 30 years later in Athens in 1896.*

His success percentage should also be mentioned (remember, as discussed in the introduction this is measured by awarding one point for a team win and half a point for a team draw in each match in which the player appears). At 68% Grace has the second highest success percentage of all the England core players featured in this book, the highest being George Lohmann.

So, who were the main pre-First World War players and how has history judged them?

1ST ERA BATSMEN

Here is a summary table of the batsmen,
with the players listed in descending order of runs scored.

		M	R	RAW AV	ADJ AV	RAW RK	ADJ RK
C HILL	AUS	41	2660	35.46	39.35	42	26
TRUMPER	AUS	40	2263	32.79	37.56	52	33
S GREGORY	AUS	52	2193	25.80	27.48	61	61
ARMSTRONG	AUS	42	2172	35.03	37.11	45	36
MACLAREN	ENG	35	1931	33.87	35.98	47	40
NOBLE	AUS	39	1905	30.72	33.52	56	47
HAYWARD	ENG	29	1747	35.65	36.30	41	38
RHODES	ENG	41	1706	31.01	33.51	54	49
J DARLING	AUS	31	1632	30.79	32.99	55	51
GRACE	ENG	22	1098	32.29	50.66	53	9

As mentioned in the introduction the qualification for batsmen to be included is 1,500 runs with an exception made for WG Grace. Where possible, all players have been included in their primary era. However there are some who featured so prominently in more than one era that this was not possible. Two players who featured prominently in both this first era and the next are England's Jack Hobbs and Australia's Charlie Macartney. The movement in their averages and rankings under the adjustment mechanism is affected by the underlying features of both periods and so both Hobbs and

Macartney are discussed below after the review of the first and second eras. (The adjustment calculation itself, of course, is not affected by the era to which players are allocated as it is a specific calculation based on the exact games in which they played). Two players from this era—Monty Noble and Wilfred Rhodes—together with Keith Miller from the third era and Ian Botham from the fourth era achieve the qualification criteria for both batting and bowling and so are discussed as all-rounders in Chapter 9.

Apart from Grace, the batsman from the first era who has been most eulogised by cricket writers through the ages is undoubtedly the Australian Victor Trumper, who scored more centuries (six) in the pre-War era than any other player. In his 2009 book *Top 100 Cricketers of All Time,* Christopher Martin Jenkins (CMJ) ranks Trumper at 30, higher than all of the above except Grace and his teammate Wilfred Rhodes, the latter owing his placing in CMJ's book more to his bowling than his batting.

When Australia toured England in 1902 Trumper scored more than 2,500 runs in first class matches, nearly 1,000 more than any other batsman (including all the English county players). Other top players of the time, spoke of him reverently. The English batsman AC MacLaren, who also features in the table above, once said to Neville Cardus, "They used to talk of my 'Grand Manner'. Compared to Victor I was like a cab horse side by side with a thoroughbred Derby winner". Trumper's teammate, Charlie Macartney said, "I should have been proud to carry his bag".

Yet because of his inconsistency the figures don't reflect Trumper's undoubted brilliance. A number of low scores dilute the impact of wonderful innings, such as 100 before lunch in the 1902 Old Trafford Test and 185 not out in the second innings at Sydney in December 1903. Perhaps the inconsistency was partly due to his ill-health; in 1907 he contracted scarlet fever and he died from Brights disease eight years later, aged just 37.

Other than Grace, it is left-hander Clem Hill rather than Trumper who has the highest ranking at 26th, seven places above Trumper. He also has the highest run aggregate of 2,660, 397 above Trumper from just one more match.

Born on the rest day of the very first Test match in 1877, Clem Hill was the first great left hander from Australia. His 188 at Melbourne in 1898 is still the highest score in Ashes Tests by a player under 21 years of age. Although he scored just four hundreds in his 41 matches he had an additional five scores in excess of 90.

He was a central figure on behalf of the players in their disputes with the newly formed Australian Board of Control between 1905 and 1912. He became a selector but fell out with Peter McAlister one of his two co-selectors and as a consequence refused to tour England in 1909. Despite captaining Australia in the Ashes series in 1911/12 Hill was in dispute again with McAlister about the upcoming tour of England in 1912 and this culminated in a physical fight between them. He then quit as a selector and he, Victor Trumper, Warwick Armstrong, 'Tibby' Cotter, Hanson Carter and Vernon Ransford, all of whom were senior players, refused to tour England in 1912. The War then intervened and Hill didn't play again for Australia.

1ST ERA BOWLERS

All the bowlers from this era suffer adverse adjustments in their averages and there are more large adjustments to raw averages than was the case with the batsmen. The adverse adjustments of course arise from the low scoring games and unsurprisingly these games were often played on poor wickets where the best bowlers would spend more time bowling (perhaps being kept on for much if not all of an innings) than the best batsmen would spend batting.

Chapter 12, which reviews the results overall and endeavours to draw conclusions, explains why I believe that the adjusted averages produce fair results for all the players including those who do suffer these large adverse adjustments, such as the era 1 bowlers.

Of the 12 bowlers who played primarily in this first era, all see the average number of runs they conceded per wicket taken increase and all except Sydney Barnes and Tom Richardson subsequently drop significantly in the rankings, the average fall being 15 places.

1ST ERA BOWLERS

Here is the list in the same format as for the batsmen:

		M	W	RAW AV	ADJ AV	RAW RK	ADJ RK
TRUMBLE	AUS	31	141	20.88	25.59	7	18
NOBLE	AUS	39	115	24.86	28.33	20	33
RHODES	ENG	41	109	24.00	27.88	17	32
S BARNES	ENG	20	106	21.58	24.86	12	15
GIFFEN	AUS	31	103	27.09	33.24	29	43
TURNER	AUS	17	101	16.53	28.65	2	37
PEEL	ENG	20	101	16.98	25.14	3	17
BRIGGS	ENG	31	97	20.55	25.72	6	20
SPOFFORTH	AUS	18	94	18.41	28.49	5	35
RICHARDSON	ENG	14	88	25.22	26.64	21	25
PALMER	AUS	17	78	21.51	27.10	11	29
LOHMANN	ENG	15	77	13.01	25.68	1	19

George Lohmann, who easily tops both the era and the overall raw averages, took his 77 wickets in low-scoring games and as a result drops 18 places. Charlie Turner and Bobby Peel, second and third respectively also fare badly. Their careers spanned a similar period (Turner from 1886 to 1894 and Peel from 1884 to 1896), they both took 101 wickets and they have similar raw averages. However, there is a large variation between them. Turner drops 35 places but Peel just 14. This is primarily because Turner took 17 wickets in the low scoring two-match series of 1886/87 when Peel didn't play and Peel took 21 wickets in the comparatively high scoring series of 1884/85 when Turner didn't play.

It should be remembered that at the time not only was pitch preparation at an early stage of development leading to generally lower scores, but also the effect of the weather could be devastating. Due to uncovered pitches, overnight rain could result in highly difficult conditions for the batsmen the following day. This was particularly so in Australia where hot sun after rain could make the wickets virtually unplayable. By way of example, the two-match series in Australia in 1886/87 had an average runs per wicket of 11.3, the single match in 1887/88 an average of 8.7 and the three-match series in England in the wet summer of 1888 an average of 10.8. Much of the bowling in this period was done by spinners, like England's Johnny Briggs and Bobby Peel and Australia's Hugh Trumble, and medium to medium-fast pacers, like England's Lohmann and Australia's Turner, although the latter two both employed spin at their faster pace.

Fred Spofforth, who probably has the strongest reputation of the early Australian bowlers is also affected badly by the adjustment mechanism, his average increasing from 18.4 to 28.5 and his ranking falling from 5th to 35th. He bowled right arm at fast medium and used the break back to great effect. At 6' 3" he was a commanding figure and was the first bowler to use eye-to-eye contact with the batsman as a technique to scare him, becoming known as the "Demon Bowler". Spofforth played in 18 Tests during a ten-year career, making his debut in the second ever Test, played in 1877 (he reputedly refused to play in the first because Jack Blackham was selected as wicketkeeper rather than Billy Murdoch).

He was certainly rated highly by his contemporaries; RH Lyttleton, writing in 1899, said he regarded Spofforth as the greatest bowler the world had ever seen[5]. George Giffen, who himself features in our list of bowlers from the first era, also regarded Spofforth as the greatest bowler of his time. However, he also wrote that: "on a batsman's wicket he was not so fine a bowler perhaps as Palmer or Boyle".

In looking at some of these early writings one can't help but feel there was a general expectation that wickets would be imperfect and favour the bowler rather than be true. Later bowlers could not expect this and have had to amend their tactics accordingly. The development of better wickets eventually led to the run spree between the wars, to "bodyline" in an effort to curb Bradman, and to the change in the LBW law all of which are discussed below. Yet the

[5]   RH Lyttleton was brother of the Hon Alfred who played four Tests for England between 1880 and 1884. Alfred's main claim to fame came at the Oval in 1884 when, despite keeping wicket, he was asked to bowl. Still wearing his pads, he sent down a series of underarm lobs and took 4-19 as Australia collapsed from 532-6 to 551 all out.

assessment of Spofforth today is still high; CMJ ranks him 27th in his all-time top 100. Don Bradman doesn't select him in his all-time Australian Ashes 12 though Geoff Boycott makes him one of three reserve bowlers for his all-time Australian squad of 13.

Perhaps Spofforth's greatest feat came in the single Test at the Oval in 1882 during which he took 14 wickets to give Australia their first win on English soil, by just 7 runs, a victory which led to the famous mock obituary of English cricket in *The Sporting Times*. Australia batted first and managed just 63. Spofforth then took 7 for 46 including the wicket of WG Grace to restrict England to 101. Australia fared only slightly better in their second innings and their score of 122 left England just 85 to win. At 51-2 it looked easy but once WG Grace and George Ulyett were out the lower order collapsed to 77 all out with Spofforth taking 7-44. It was Spofforth more than any other member of the Australian team who was convinced throughout that they could win.

He wasn't always as successful. In 1882/83, the series after which the Melbourne ladies presented the Ashes urn to Ivo Bligh, Spofforth took four wickets a little expensively in the first match, took none for 57 in the second and three wickets fairly expensively in the added, fourth match. It was only in the third when he achieved 11 for 117 that he really succeeded and even that was not enough to prevent England winning by 69 runs.

Similarly, in the three-match series in England in 1886 his six wickets in the first Test were eclipsed by Barlow's eight much more cheaply for England. In the second Test Spofforth was unable to prevent Shrewsbury scoring a match-winning innings of 164 on a rain-affected pitch on which Briggs then took 11 wickets to dismiss Australia twice cheaply. In the following game, he was unable to prevent WG Grace making 170 to lead England to a score of 434 and an innings victory, Lohmann doing the main damage for England as Australia were dismissed twice for a combined total of just 217.

Overall this meant that in pure figures he did his bowling in games which had some of the lowest scores ever recorded and his overall raw average of 18.41 was only marginally lower than the average runs per wicket in the games he played. It is this that leads to his increased adjusted average and his lowly place in the rankings.

By contrast, Tom Richardson, one of England's first genuine fast bowlers, who is considered to have inspired the Australians to concentrate more on developing fast bowlers, played his Tests in the 1890s when pitch conditions had improved considerably. Particularly impressive is his strike rate of wickets per match played, which at 6.29, is the best of all the featured bowlers across all the eras.

Sydney Barnes, considered by most of his contemporaries to be the greatest bowler of them all, played his Tests against Australia between 1901 and 1912. He bowled right-arm at fast-medium pace but in the words of John Arlott had the accuracy, spin and resource of a slow bowler. Barnes considered himself a spin bowler as he bowled both the off break and the leg break. By the time he was playing, pitch conditions were consistently better and all the series played from 1901 up to 1912, the last before WWI, had an average figure for runs per wicket of more than 20, with the 1905 series in England and the 1911/12 series in Australia averaging above 29.

Barnes and Richardson were the only two bowlers to feature in *The Six Giants of the Wisden Century* selected by Neville Cardus for the almanack's 100th edition published in 1963. Barnes was also rated No 7 in CMJ's book of the 100 all-time top players as well as being included in both Don Bradman's best English team of all time, chosen in 2000, and Geoff Boycott's, chosen in 2008, with Boycott making him the number one pick of the England bowlers.

For much of his career Barnes chose to play league cricket rather than first class cricket in the County Championship, due to its higher financial rewards. It was not until the late summer of 1901 when Barnes was already 28 that Archie MacLaren persuaded him to play in Lancashire's final county game of the season against Leicestershire and then to tour Australia that winter under his captaincy.

Although Barnes took 6 for 99 in that game against Leicestershire, in the only five previous county games he'd played, between 1895 and 1899, he had taken just seven wickets at a cost of 360 runs. However, MacLaren, who desperately wanted to win back the Ashes which he had failed to do in 1899, was prepared to take the risk because Yorkshire's star bowlers Wilfred Rhodes and George Hirst had been prevented from touring Australia by Lord Hawke who was then both Captain and President of Yorkshire.

Barnes bowled England to victory in the first Test with 5-65 in the first innings, including the wickets of Trumper, Clem Hill and Joe Darling. He then took 13 wickets in the second Test but Australia still managed to win by 229 runs. He broke down in the third Test probably from over-bowling and didn't play in the last two games which England lost, handing Australia a 4-1 series victory.

Perhaps because of his greater economic independence (he could go back to league cricket and in fact did so after two years of County Championship cricket in 1902 and 1903) Barnes never had the same deference to the amateur players and the cricket establishment of the time as other professionals. This caused a number of disputes, mainly financial, and apart from one match in 1902 he played no more Test cricket until the 1907/08 tour to Australia when he was 34 years of age. Twenty-four wickets during that tour were followed by 17 in 1909 (from just 3 matches) and 34 in 1911/12. England lost the 1907/08 series 4-1 to a strong Australian side which included Trumper, Armstrong, Hill, Noble and Macartney. The selectors, led by Lord Hawke, didn't choose Barnes until the third game of the 1909 series which Australia won to take the series 2-1, the last two games being drawn, and it was not until the 1911-12 series that Barnes was able to deliver a series victory for England.

Barnes did not bowl well in the first Test, perhaps out of pique after captain JWHT Douglas had taken the new ball himself rather than giving it to Barnes. However, after losing that game, England won the next four with Barnes taking eight wickets in each of the second and third Tests and seven wickets in each of the fourth and fifth. The fourth Test was notable for the 323-run opening partnership between Hobbs and Rhodes, the highest first wicket partnership for England against Australia.

If Barnes had been more accommodating during his career and the selectors more even-handed in their selection and in their management of him, he would have had many more wickets. As it is, his Ashes figures, strong though they are, do not properly reflect his true standing. Of the 41 bowlers featured across all the eras he ranks 12th in the raw averages and 15th in the adjusted averages.

Although Barnes' ranking is not as high as one might expect from his reputation, the adjustment mechanism, in moving him down just three places, treats him much more kindly than many others from that first era. This is because he did his bowling in the higher scoring games of the early 1900s rather than the much lower scoring games of the 1880s and 1890s.

1920 TO 1938

Among the many first class cricketers who lost their lives in the First World War were three Ashes Test cricketers, Colin Blythe and Kenneth Hutchings from England, and 'Tibby' Cotter, discussed briefly in Chapter 8, from Australia. After the horrors of the war it was a further two years before the Ashes rivalry was revived and it began with a period of domination for Australia who won the first eight tests. In the first series, in 1920/21 in Australia, Warwick Armstrong captained a fine home side with the first pair of opening bowlers, Jack Gregory and Ted McDonald, which bore resemblance to the opening attacks seen today. England's batting, Hobbs and Douglas apart, fared badly and their bowling, known to be weak, never posed anything like the threat the Australians possessed. The result was the first whitewash in a five-match series, a feat not repeated in the Ashes until 2006/07. The series in England in 1921 was not much better for the hosts, with Australia winning the first three tests and the final two being drawn.

All tests in Australia during this inter-war era were played to a finish no matter how long that took, and the first three games in 1924/25 were won by Australia over seven days. England managed to win the fourth, their first victory over Australia since the war (and the only match in the series where they won the toss and batted first) but lost again in the final Test at Sydney.

In contrast, Tests in England at this time were played over just three days but in 1926 it was agreed, for the first time, that the final match of the series would be played to a finish. McDonald was no longer playing and Gregory who was nearing the end of his career took just three wickets in the series. With rain ruining the first Test, and three days proving insufficient generally to achieve a result, the first four Tests were drawn but England achieved a famous victory in four days in the final test at the Oval. Hobbs and Sutcliffe both scored centuries in the second innings on a rain-affected wicket, and Wilfred Rhodes, recalled at 48 years old, took 4-44 in Australia's second innings.

By the time they toured Australia in the winter of 1928/29, England were in the ascendancy. Wally Hammond scored 905 runs, a record series aggregate at the time, and still the record for an Englishman. Hobbs and Sutcliffe were still there and Maurice Tate, Harold Larwood, Jack White and George Geary handled the bowling admirably. The result was a 4-1 series win for England although Don Bradman, who played four games in his debut series (he was dropped for the second game), provided a glimpse of things to come.

In 1930 Bradman dominated proceedings with a record series tally of 974 runs. The enormity of this achievement is demonstrated by the fact that not only does it remain a record today, but no one other than Hammond in the 1928/29 series has got within 130 runs of it (despite there having been a number of six-match series played). Test matches in England ran to four days now and the hosts won the first Test at Trent Bridge, before losing the second at Lord's. The next two were drawn but Australia clinched the series decider at the Oval, a 'timeless' Test which ran to six days (one day being lost to rain), by an innings and 39 runs.

England regained the Ashes with a 4-1 series win Down Under in 1932/33. However, the tour will forever be remembered for the Bodyline controversy in which England's opening bowling attack, under Douglas Jardine's captaincy, targeted the leg stump rather than the off stump as was traditional. With a predominantly leg side field batsmen were, as they defended themselves, at risk of fending off short pitched balls into the hands of the waiting short leg fielders. Under Jardine's direction the Nottinghamshire pair of Larwood and Bill Voce were the chief exponents of the strategy although Gubby Allen, who refused to bowl Bodyline, also had success as did spinner Hedley Verity. England's tactics on this tour aroused more emotion and controversy than any tour before or since.

The fallout meant that Jardine, Larwood and Voce were all absent in 1934 and England were captained by Bob Wyatt who had been opposed to Bodyline. Bradman didn't really make a mark until the fourth Test at Headingley, where he made 304 not out. He followed that with 244 at the Oval, although that was surpassed by Bill Ponsford, who scored 266. The pair put on 451 for the second wicket, which remained unbeaten in Test cricket for 56 years, helping the visitors to win by 562 runs and seal the series 2-1.

By 1936/37 Bradman had taken over as captain for Australia and Allen for England. Rain-affected pitches and the bowling of Allen and Voce helped England win the first two games by large margins. In the third Test it was England's turn to be caught out by a rain-affected pitch. Bradman successfully inverted the batting order in the second innings to protect the leading Australian batsmen from the worst of the pitch, scoring 270 himself in a return to form. Another Bradman double century and ten wickets from Fleetwood Smith secured victory in the fourth match for Australia and in the final Test Bradman, McCabe and Jack Badcock all made centuries to help Australia to a total of more than 600, and an innings victory. It remains the only time in Ashes history that a series has been won by a team that had lost the first two tests.

In 1938, the first two Tests were drawn and the third, at Old Trafford, was washed out without a ball being bowled (one of only three occasions in Ashes history this has happened, the other two being at Old Trafford in 1890 and Melbourne in 1970/71). Australia won the fourth Test at Headingley by five wickets after O'Reilly took 10-122, England struggling to reach 123 in their second innings with no one reaching 30. The final match, at the Oval, was another timeless Test. England won the toss and on an easy paced wicket they made a record Ashes score of 903-7 declared[6]. In the process Len Hutton broke Bradman's record individual Ashes score with a knock of 364, setting a record which also remains today[7]. Initially England's captain Wally Hammond had aimed to score more than 1,000 as he was concerned that Australia, led by Bradman, would be able to make a massive score in return, on what was a true, long

[6]   *At the time it was the record Test score and it has only been surpassed by Sri Lanka, who made 952/6d against India in 1997.*

[7]   *Hutton's score was also a record Test score at the time. It stood for 20 years until Garfield Sobers scored 365 for the West indies against Pakistan in 1958.*

lasting, easy paced wicket. However Bradman wrenched an ankle when trying his luck as a bowler and was unable to take any further part in the match. On hearing this Hammond declared and England came home to win by an innings and 579 runs, another Ashes record which remains today. However it still meant that England had only drawn the series and so the Ashes stayed with Australia.

At 34.3, the average runs per wicket during this era was the highest of all the five eras and generally it is considered to be a time when batsmen dominated. Certainly, the advances in pitch preparation gave batsmen an advantage over their predecessors in the first era. Second era batsmen also had an advantage over those in later periods because of the LBW law which only changed in 1935 (initially on an experimental basis, with the change becoming permanent in 1937). Prior to 1935 a batsman could not be out LBW to a ball pitching outside the off stump.

This imbalance between bat and ball is reflected in the fact that, although it is the shortest era, (49 matches only), nine of the 61 batsmen featured in this book played primarily in this second era whereas only four of the 43 bowlers did so. Another indicator is that the records for series run aggregates in England and Australia both occurred in this era; Bradman for a series in England (974 in 1930) and Hammond for a series in Australia (905 in 1928/29).

Bodyline was an aggressive attempt by England to reduce such batting dominance, and in particular that of Don Bradman, on their tour Down Under in 1932/33 and it is worth noting that the series has the lowest runs per wicket for the era at just 28.4.

Given the average runs per wicket for the era of 34.3 it is to be expected that the adjustments to raw batting averages and to batting rankings will be downwards and this is indeed the case. All the nine featured batsmen have lower adjusted averages and all save Bradman who retains his number 1 slot drop in the overall rankings.

2ND ERA BATSMEN

The figures for the nine players are:

	🏳	M	R	RAW AV	ADJ AV	RAW RK	ADJ RK
BRADMAN	AUS	37	5028	89.78	73.73	1	1
HAMMOND	ENG	33	2852	51.85	42.89	10	20
SUTCLIFFE	ENG	27	2741	66.85	56.42	2	3
MCCABE	AUS	24	1931	48.27	39.84	16	24
HENDREN	ENG	28	1740	39.55	31.64	34	56
LEYLAND	ENG	20	1705	56.83	49.15	6	12
WOODFULL	AUS	25	1675	44.07	34.03	26	44
WOOLLEY	ENG	32	1664	33.28	32.13	50	54
PONSFORD	AUS	20	1558	47.21	38.70	18	30

It is only right to talk here about Bradman whose status as the leading batsman of all time is undisputed. He was born in New South Wales into a farming family in 1908 and soon moved to Bowral just 50 miles from Sydney. As a young boy he would while away the hours by using a stump to hit a golf ball at a water tank behind the family home. When the ball rebounded Bradman would attempt to hit it again, in the process honing his timing and reactions. A cricket bat and ball must have seemed very easy after this.

At the age of 19 he was playing Sheffield Shield cricket and a year later in 1928 he made his Test debut, against England, at Brisbane's Exhibition Ground (this was one of only two Tests played at the venue, the other against the West Indies in 1931, before international matches moved to the "Gabba"). England won by 675 runs with Bradman scoring 18 and 1. He was dropped for the second Test but returned for the third and missed only one more game against England (due to illness) until the end of his career in 1948.

There was no magical factor to explain the extent of Bradman's superiority and he was certainly not the most attractive batsman to watch. Others from across the eras, such as Victor Trumper, Wally Hammond and David Gower have exuded more artistry. However, what Bradman did possess was a strong discipline which accentuated his superior judgment, eyesight and reaction time. His discipline meant he did not indulge himself by playing unnecessarily stylish shots so as to communicate his superiority. Such indulgence would have been wholly foreign to Bradman. He was quiet, undemonstrative, meticulous and introspective though ruthless in execution.

For Bradman batting was a science where the objective was simply to score runs. He had exceptional technique, concentration and an ability to see the ball early. He used these tools efficiently to achieve that objective. He had all the shots in his armoury and so could use them at will, according to the circumstances. He took no unnecessary risks and so hit few sixes; hitting the ball in the air created an unnecessary risk of being caught. For Bradman, reaching 50 was not a milestone in the way it was to lesser players. He converted 61% of the 50s he made into centuries, or more, a much higher percentage than for other batsmen, though Steve Smith with 55% currently is not far behind. (The only featured batsman to have more success in turning 50s into 100s was Maurice Leyland whose record against Australia was much superior to his overall Test record which in turn was much superior to his general first class record). Bradman knew exactly what he was capable of and had the discipline to execute it perfectly. He had no temptation or necessity to overreach himself.

An exception to this normal, controlled approach was when England employed Bodyline on their tour to Australia in 1932/33. The fast leg theory attack spearheaded by Larwood and Voce was developed at least partly because it was thought Bradman might have a weakness against it. Sometimes he tried to counteract it by moving a long way to leg and forcing shots through the skeleton off-side field. These were risky shots and he got out to them on a number of occasions. His adjusted average for that series at 62.63 (his raw average was 56.57) was lower than his overall adjusted average.

Bradman suffers by being compared with high averages to which he has contributed and his average falls from a raw figure of 89.78 (the figure of 99.94 that everyone seems to know was for Tests against *all* countries) to 73.73. Sutcliffe, the next highest in this era drops from 66.85 to 56.42. With Steve Smith now second overall at 57.52 Bradman has an overall lead over any other batsman even after the figures are adjusted of a sizeable 28 per cent.

Furthermore, he scored eight of the 26 double centuries notched up by Australia in 142 years of Ashes history (England only have 14 in total). He scored 19 hundreds, the next highest being 12 for Hobbs, then 10 for Steve Waugh, despite playing four fewer Ashes Tests than Hobbs and nine fewer than Waugh. Included in his eight double centuries were two triple centuries, both at Leeds in 1930 and 1934. Only three other triple centuries have ever been made in Ashes cricket. Furthermore, Bradman recorded four of the 12 highest individual series aggregates in Ashes history and he shares in five of the record wicket partnerships for Australia against England, for the second, third, fourth, fifth and sixth wickets. I could go on.

Which were Bradman's best innings? One can do no better than to look at the great man's own opinion expressed in Roland Perry's book *Bradman's Best Ashes Teams*. His top five (all double centuries) in order were:

1.   254 at Lord's in 1930
2.   304 at Leeds in 1934
3.   334 at Leeds in 1930
4.   270 at Melbourne in 1936/37
5.   244 at the Oval in 1934

It is interesting to note that all five were pre-war innings (he was 38 when the first post-war series was played) and that four of them were in England. His innings at Lord's in 1930, which took just 339 minutes, helped Australia to their record score against England of 729 for 6 and victory by seven wickets, England having previously won the opening match of the series at Trent Bridge. This was a chanceless innings with hardly an error and laid the basis for Australia's victory in the match and subsequently by 2-1 in the series. Interestingly, neither of Bradman's two triple centuries resulted in match wins for Australia, both games being drawn. (In fact only one of the five triple centuries in Ashes tests, Len Hutton's 364 in 1938, has resulted in a win - the other four games have been drawn).

As mentioned above, his innings of 270 at Melbourne came after the tail-enders had gone in first and Bradman went in at No 7 with the score at 97 for 5. It was a key moment for Bradman in his first test series as captain, relatively out of form and with England leading the series 2-0. A run-saving field slowed his normally fast scoring rate but his partnership of 346 with Jack Fingleton set up an Australian victory by 365 runs. The innings of 244 at the Oval in 1934 was part of the record 2nd wicket partnership of 451 with Bill Ponsford which took Australia to 701 and victory in the deciding match of the series. His innings lasted only five and a quarter hours at a strike rate of 89.9 runs per 100 balls.

After Bradman others seem merely human but many of those with the strongest reputations also played in this era. Present in most preferred England all time teams is Wally Hammond, who also suffers from the high Era 2 benchmark. His raw average of 51.85 falls to an adjusted average of 42.89 and he falls from tenth to 20th in the rankings. Hammond scored four of England's 14 double hundreds, no one else having scored more than two and with nine centuries is, along with David Gower who played more matches, joint second behind Jack Hobbs, who scored 12, in the England figures. We'll talk more about Hammond in Chapter 14, when we look at the all-time best teams.

* * *

Before looking at the second era bowlers, there are two batsmen whose careers were split between the first and second eras and who should be discussed separately: England's Jack Hobbs and Australia's Charlie Macartney. The former played 15 Ashes Tests before World War One and 26 in the inter-war period, while the latter played 14 before the Great War and 12 between the wars. You can see their respective statistics in the table below.

HOBBS & MACARTNEY

		M	R	RAW AV	ADJ AV	RAW RK	ADJ RK
HOBBS	ENG	41	3636	54.26	50.26	9	10
MACARTNEY	AUS	26	1640	43.15	40.19	27	23

These are two very interesting players to analyse. Hobbs is considered by many to be the greatest ever English batsman and is ranked five by CMJ in his top cricketers of all time, the only Englishman above him being WG Grace. He is ninth in the raw averages and tenth in the adjusted averages.

Known universally as The Master, Hobbs is the leading scorer of first class centuries, with 197, and of first class runs with 61,237. He first played for Surrey at age 22 and for England at age 25. He was 38 when the first post-World War One Test was played and he carried on playing Tests for another nine years. In fact 132 of his 197 centuries were scored after the Armistice. Yet he himself said: "I was never the player after the war that I was before. I couldn't be, I couldn't play the strokes, I was too old".

As you can see in the table below, a comparison of Hobbs' pre-war and inter-war Ashes performances certainly seems to bear out his own comments. Although his raw average is similar in the two periods, the adjustment would put him comfortably in second place to Bradman overall based on his pre-war performances but in a more lowly 19th based on his inter-war ones.

HOBBS, PRE-WAR & POST-WAR

	M	R	RAW AV	ADJ AV	RAW RK	ADJ RK
TO 1912	15	1320	55.00	62.57	9	2
FROM 1920	26	2316	53.86	43.40	9	19

It must be questionable how informative it is to divide a batsman's career in this way though Hobbs's case is a distinctive one because of his prominence and the eight year gap in Ashes cricket caused by the war. But there are many batsmen who have had periods of differing effectiveness. A number of players have had very low scores for a period before adjusting fully to international cricket, while some have carried on too long and had many low scores towards the end of their careers. One can't adjust for this - one can only take all the scores that any batsman makes.

Hobbs's case though may give us a little insight into how we assess cricketers. Clearly we allocate considerable value to qualities that don't find their way into averages at all, and rightly so. We also attach weight to superior scores even if the player's other scores dilute their overall average. So, a player who scores 10 swashbuckling centuries resulting in victories for his side but who has 10 ducks elsewhere in his career seems more exciting, and of more value, than a player who achieves the same average courtesy of 20 solid half centuries. It is interesting that in the 15 matches Hobbs played before the war there were nine centuries scored by England batsmen and Hobbs scored four of these. In his 26 post-war matches there were 28 England centuries and Hobbs scored eight, very creditable but a much lower proportion than before the war, one illustration of how much more dependent England were on him in that earlier period. Is our lasting memory of Hobbs as The Master, driven by his pre-war performances which we've separated in our minds from his merely excellent post war scores? This is further complicated by the fact that the raw averages were almost the same but in the post-war years many others had high averages as well.

Charlie Macartney held the record for the most runs scored by one batsman in a single day in first class cricket for more than seventy years. The 345 he scored for Australia against Notts in 1921 was not surpassed until 1994, when Brian Lara batting for Warwickshire against Durham on the final day of the match added 390 to his overnight score of 111 not out. (In doing so he eclipsed not only Macartney's record tally for a day but also set a new record for the highest individual score in any first class match of 501 not out). Macartney's aggressive stroke play, which is the quality most remembered in the writings of those who saw him, seems to have come into his play after the war. Before 1914 his batting performances were patchy and often his bowling was more successful. After the war he played some truly explosive innings with his 151 against England in the Headingley Test of 1926 considered by many to be the finest innings they ever saw. The passage of time has undoubtedly diluted the memory of him and he just makes it into CMJ's listing at number 100. Bradman himself however, in Roland Perry's book published in 2002, includes him at No 5 in the batting order for his top Australian Ashes team of all time and ranks his 170 in the fifth Test at Sydney in 1920/21 as one of the five (non-Bradman) top innings he saw in Ashes matches.

2ND ERA BOWLERS

The shortness of the era and the dominance of the batsmen mean that only four bowlers who played primarily in this era have achieved the qualifying condition of 75 wickets.

These bowlers are:

	⚑	M	W	RAW AV	ADJ AV	RAW RK	ADJ RK
GRIMMETT	AUS	22	106	32.44	26.99	40	28
O'REILLY	AUS	19	102	25.36	23.24	23	7
MAILEY	AUS	18	86	34.12	27.39	41	31
TATE	ENG	20	83	30.60	23.74	37	8

All four are elevated in the rankings by the adjustment, not surprisingly in view of the high runs conceded per wicket taken of 35.7 in this era, with Australia's Bill O' Reilly the leader. Known as The Tiger, his leg spin was bowled at medium pace with an aggressive manner more resembling a fast bowler and he did have a faster ball that was genuinely quick. His leg break didn't turn as much as some but it was enough to beat the bat and he put more spin on the top spinner and wrong'un. He extracted tremendous bounce and this together with his height (6'1"), a 12-pace run-up and the flailing arms of his action gave an aggressive flavour to every delivery. Ranked at 23 by CMJ in his all-time top 100 and included by Boycott in his all-time Australian Ashes squad of 13, O'Reilly was also acknowledged by Bradman who rated him the greatest bowler he ever played against. His overall adjusted ranking of seventh makes him the third best spinner behind only Jim Laker and Shane Warne.

Maurice Tate is the only fast bowler among the four and he began as an off break bowler in the mould of his father Fred who played a single Test for England in 1902. Tate had the capacity to bowl the occasional extremely fast break back and was encouraged, particularly by his county captain Arthur Gilligan, to change over to pace on a permanent basis. He and Gilligan formed a formidable opening attack for Sussex and England until in 1924 Gilligan was struck on the heart by a delivery while batting, an injury from which he never fully recovered.

Gilligan's decreased effectiveness meant that Tate had inadequate pace support during the tour to Australia in the winter of 1924/25 which the hosts won 4-1. Tate was nevertheless England's leading bowler taking seven or more wickets in every Test other than the third when he suffered a blistered foot. His 38-wicket tally for the series is still a record for England in a Test series in Australia.

In the rankings based on adjusted averages he is eighth, the second highest Englishman behind only Jim Laker, making Tate the highest ranked England pace bowler ahead of the likes of John Snow at 13th, Fred Trueman at 24th, Stuart Broad at 30th, Ian Botham at 34th, and Bob Willis at 38th It also puts him ahead of Sydney Barnes at 15th who is still ranked by some as the greatest English bowler ever. Yet Tate is not included by Bradman or Boycott in their all-time teams and is ranked just 77th by CMJ. It appears posterity has underrated him.

1946 TO THE 1977 CENTENARY TEST

This era, which runs from the resumption of Ashes Tests after World War Two until the Centenary Test in 1977, just before Kerry Packer's controversial intervention into cricket, was notable for the dominance of the Australians who won 31 of the 82 Test matches played compared to just 16 victories for England, the remaining 35 games being drawn. Four Ashes Test cricketers lost their lives in the war, Ken Farnes, George Macaulay and Hedley Verity of England and Ross Gregory of Australia. Verity is discussed in Chapter 8.

Following the war, the Australian policy of playing timeless Tests was discontinued. Instead they were played across six five-hour days making them equal in duration with matches in England, which were now to be played across five six-hour days.

Bradman played in just the first two series after the war, in Australia in 1946/47 and in England in 1948. He was ably supported in the batting line up by Arthur Morris and Sid Barnes while Ray Lindwall and Keith Miller soon formed the most hostile and effective Australian fast bowling attack since Jack Gregory and Ted McDonald. England still had Len Hutton and Denis Compton, and in 1946/47 Wally Hammond, but the bowling was too dependent on Alec Bedser.

In that first series, Down Under, Australia won the first two Tests by more than an innings after they had racked up scores of more than 600. England improved in the third Test but could not force more than a draw (the first Test in Australia not to produce a result since 1881/82). Hutton and Compton could only muster a single 50 between them in the first three Tests but both returned to form at Adelaide for the fourth Test, with Compton getting centuries in both innings and Hutton notching half centuries. England got to a position where they were able to declare and set Australia a fourth innings target of 314 but the game was left drawn with Australia only one wicket down. In the final Test, Hutton's enforced retirement, in the first innings and absence in the second, due to tonsillitis, contributed to England's defeat by five wickets, giving Australia a 3-0 series win.

Bradman's touring side of 1948 is widely considered, even today, as the strongest Australian side in history. England lost the first two tests by large margins. Hutton, who had struggled against the Australian short-pitched bowling, was controversially dropped for the third Test. Compton scored 145 not out to help set a target of 317, but rain meant the game ended a draw. Hutton returned for the fourth Test and scored two half centuries, and a strong all-round batting performance put England in a position where they were able to declare and set Australia 404 to win. However, Laker, the only specialist spinner in the England line up, was unable to take advantage of a slow turning wicket. Some dropped catches and scores of 182 by Morris and 173 by Bradman gave Australia victory by seven wickets. Australia's total of 404/3 was, until 1976, the highest fourth innings winning total in all Tests and it remains the highest for Ashes Tests. It was the first occasion in Ashes history that a target set by a third innings declaration was successfully attained by the side batting last. This feat was unmatched until 2001 when, also at Headingley, England successfully reached 315 for 4 to win by six wickets, a match discussed below.

In the final test at the Oval, the last of Bradman's career, England collapsed to 52 all out, their lowest score since the record low of 45 at Sydney in 1887 (when the pitch had been used earlier that same morning for another match). Hutton, last out, made 30. In unchanged conditions Australia put on 117 for the first wicket before Bradman came in to be bowled by Eric Hollies for a duck[8]. This proved to be Bradman's last Test innings as England were dismissed cheaply in the second innings to lose the match by an innings and 149 runs and the series by 4-0.

---

[8] *If Bradman had scored just four runs he would have finished his career with an overall Test average of 100.*

England could have won the first two tests in 1950/51 if they had had a little more luck and taken their chances but as it was they went to the fifth Test 4-0 down before managing finally to secure their first victory against Australia since the Oval test of 1938.

In the Coronation year of 1953 history was made with England appointing a professional, Len Hutton, as captain in an Ashes series for the first time since Arthur Shrewsbury in 1886/87. The first four matches were drawn and England won the fifth through the bowling of Alec Bedser and Fred Trueman in the first innings and Jim Laker and Tony Lock in the second. Bedser finished with a series aggregate of 39, still the highest tally for an England pace bowler in an Ashes series and the highest for a pace bowler on either side if six-match series are excluded.

England now held the Ashes for the first time since 1933 but their first defence in Australia in 1954/55 began badly. Australia amassed 600 after Hutton had put them in to bat, perhaps having over-estimated the effect of new rules in Australia which allowed full covering of the pitch for the first time. England lost by an innings but recovered to win the next three Tests and take the series 3-1 thanks to the bowling of Frank Tyson, supported by Brian Statham, and the batting of Peter May and Colin Cowdrey. Tyson took 28 wickets in the series with some of the fastest bowling ever seen in Australia. His 6-85 in the second innings at Sydney came after he had been felled by a Lindwall bouncer and he followed this with 7-27 at Melbourne in the third Test. However, he was beset by injury for much of his later career and played only three more Ashes Tests.

Following Hutton's retirement in 1956, May was appointed captain. He led England to a 2-1 victory in the home series thanks largely to an Ashes record series tally of 46 wickets from off spinner Jim Laker, which included the record match figures of 19 for 90 at Old Trafford.

Although they were favourites in Australia in 1958/59 England's batting and bowling disappointed in a generally dull series and Australia regained the Ashes with a 4-0 win. The scoring rate in this series was astonishingly slow. Overall, England achieved a rate of 2.66 runs per over but these were eight-ball overs which were used in Australia until 1978/79. That's equivalent to just about two runs per over for a six-ball over or a strike rate of 33 per 100 balls. Australia were a little better with a strike rate of 42. In England's second innings of 198 at Brisbane the rate was just 23 runs per 100 balls and Trevor Bailey took five hours and 57 minutes to reach 50. Not only does this remain the slowest half century in Ashes cricket, but also in all first class cricket.

England's scoring in 1961 was not quite so bad, thanks in large part to Dexter's aggressive batting. After a draw in the first Test, a century from Bill Lawry and the bowling of Alan Davidson and Graham McKenzie won the second for Australia at Lord's. In the following Test at Headingley, Trueman took 11 for 88 to square the series for England. On the last afternoon of the fourth Test, England began their second innings needing 256 to win with just under four hours to play. After two hours they had reached 150/1 thanks in large part to Dexter's 76 not out and the prospects looked good for them to take a series lead. But Benaud, bowling round the wicket into Trueman's footmarks, brought about a collapse. He took 6 for 70 and England lost the match by 54 runs. Australia secured a 2-1 series victory with a draw in the final Test at the Oval.

Dexter was captain for the tour to Australia in 1962/63 and had a mission to play brighter cricket and to recapture the Ashes. The England strike rate went up a little, to nearly 40 runs per hundred balls, still not very high but broadly the same as Australia's. However, success again eluded the tourists, the series being drawn 1-1. Yet another dull series, the weather contributing, followed in 1964, with Australia winning the third Test and the other four being drawn, including the fourth Test at Old Trafford. Knowing that a draw would lead to them retaining the Ashes, Australia batted until they reached 656/8 before declaring, with Simpson making 311. England scored 611 in their reply with Ken Barrington making 256 and Dexter 174.

Mike Smith captained the England side that toured Australia in 1965/66 with a similar mission to Ted Dexter's three years earlier. Another drawn series saw Australia retain the Ashes again but more attractive batting by England, epitomised by Bob Barber's 185 at Sydney, won them more friends than any touring side since Len Hutton's in 1954/55. Batsmen from both teams dominated. Bill

Lawry scored three centuries, Ken Barrington, John Edrich and Doug Walters scored two each. Bob Cowper notched 307 at Melbourne and Simpson scored 225 at Adelaide. Peter Burge and Colin Cowdrey joined Bob Barber with a single century each.

In 1968 the weather again contributed to a dull series which was drawn one game apiece, England squaring the series in the final game at the Oval with five minutes to spare as Derek Underwood finished with 7-50 in the innings.

Ray Illingworth, preferred by the selectors to Colin Cowdrey, led the English tour to Australia in 1970/71. Some English critics thought Cowdrey should have been chosen and there were many critics also in Australia, including Don Bradman who thought his field placing was negative and weighted too much to the legside. Fine batting, led by Boycott with an average of 94 and ably supported by Edrich and Brian Luckhurst, together with 31 wickets from Snow, produced a deserved 2-0 series win and the return of the Ashes to England for the first time in 12 years. This series saw the first ever Test at Perth and the first official one day international which was organised when what would have been the third test at Melbourne was abandoned without play because of continuous rain over the first three days.

England retained the Ashes at home in 1972 in a series drawn 2-2. Notable events included the emergence of Dennis Lillee taking a then series record for Australia in England of 31 wickets and Bob Massie's incredible swing bowling resulting in match figures of 16-137 on his test debut at Lord's. No other Australian bowler has even taken 15 wickets in an Ashes Test with only Fred Spofforth coming close with his 14-90 at the Oval in 1882, the match which gave birth to the Ashes. After the series against England Massie played two more Tests later that year, against Pakistan, and never played Test cricket again due to health problems. Derek Underwood's bowling in the fourth Test at Leeds gave England a series lead though Australia squared matters at the Oval thanks to a 200 partnership in the first innings by Ian and Greg Chappell and ten wickets from Lillee.

Boycott was absent from the tour to Australia in 1974/75 having said a month before the start that he would be unable to do justice to himself. The relatively unknown youngster Jeff Thomson paired with Lillee to form one of the fastest opening bowler partnerships in Ashes history. They defined the six-Test series with Lillee taking 25 wickets, and Thomson taking 30 despite missing the final match through injury. Cowdrey had to be flown out after the first Test in which both Denis Amiss and Edrich received hand fractures. England recovered to win the last Test when Thomson was unable to play but lost the series 4-1.

The England series in 1975 was arranged late, taking the opportunity that arose because Australia were in England for the first Cricket World Cup. In the continued absence of Boycott, England's batting looked fragile but Lillee and Thomson were not quite the irresistible force they had been on the faster Australian wickets, though they still took 37 wickets between them in the four-match series. A closer battle resulted in a 1-0 win for Australia.

The first 100 years of cricket between England and Australia was celebrated in March 1977 with the Centenary Test in Melbourne, the venue of the first test in 1877. Despite a rousing 174 by Derek Randall in the second innings, 11 wickets from Lillee saw Australia home by 45 runs. By an incredible coincidence this was exactly the same result as in the first match 100 years earlier. However, even as the Centenary Test was being played, cricket's next chapter was already being written. The Australian media entrepreneur Kerry Packer was contracting many of the world's leading players, including nearly all the top Australians, to his own series of matches.

3RD ERA BATSMEN

Because the overall average runs per wicket during this era, at 29.9, was close to the overall Ashes average of 28.9 we see batsmen move both up and down in the adjusted average rankings (according to whether the average in the matches they themselves played was above or below the overall average of 28.9). It is also the era with the highest number of batsmen featured—14 of the 61. Ten of our 43 featured bowlers played primarily in this era, while a further four batsmen and four bowlers had careers covering both the third and fourth eras.

3RD ERA BATSMEN

The results for the batsmen were:

	🏳	M	R	RAW AV	ADJ AV	RAW RK	ADJ RK
J EDRICH	ENG	32	2644	48.96	44.94	14	15
COWDREY	ENG	43	2433	34.26	35.05	46	43
HUTTON	ENG	27	2428	56.46	54.21	7	4
HARVEY	AUS	37	2416	38.34	42.89	38	21
LAWRY	AUS	29	2233	48.54	41.43	15	22
I CHAPPELL	AUS	30	2138	41.11	37.26	30	35
BARRINGTON	ENG	23	2111	63.96	51.07	4	7
MORRIS	AUS	24	2080	50.73	48.02	11	13
WALTERS	AUS	36	1981	35.38	33.02	44	50
COMPTON	ENG	28	1842	42.83	38.36	28	31
HASSETT	AUS	24	1572	38.34	39.24	39	27
MAY	ENG	21	1566	46.05	53.88	19	5
REDPATH	AUS	23	1512	38.76	36.09	36	39
MILLER	AUS	29	1511	33.57	33.67	48	46

The main upwards movements are for Neil Harvey, Lindsay Hassett and Peter May, all of whom played mainly in the relatively low scoring games in the 1950s. May, along with Len Hutton and Ken Barrington, features in the top ten batsmen based on adjusted rankings. Arthur Morris is at number 13. Of these, Morris and Hutton feature in both Bradman's and Boycott's top Ashes teams for Australia and England, while May is included in Bradman's team but not in Boycott's. Hutton is ranked most highly of all the batsmen in this era by CMJ, featuring at number 17 in his top 100 cricketers. However, Barrington is not included either by Bradman or Boycott and is listed at only 46 by CMJ. Both Bradman and Boycott also include Harvey and Denis Compton in their Ashes teams, although they are much lower in the adjusted rankings at 21 and 31 respectively. What does this tell us?

It surely emphasises that in making our subjective choices we do attach a great deal of weight to charisma, to a few truly match winning performances and to standing firm for the side when others are failing. Conversely, less weight is given to steady, consistent strong performances. So we rate Hutton and May highly for their many performances which were match-winning or match-saving and for standing firm when others failed. We rate Compton highly for his ability to play incredible innings against the odds, his fighting spirit, his unusual shots despite his comparatively low adjusted ranking (interestingly his overall raw Test average of 50.06 is much higher than his raw Ashes average of 42.83). Even his weaknesses, such as his poor running between the wickets and general disorganisation, added to his charisma. Harvey also had a raw Ashes average, at 38.34, that was well below his overall test average of 48.41, which goes some way to explaining his high rating by critics and contemporaries alike. But as with Compton it is not just the figures. Boycott chose Harvey for his attacking flair and Bradman, who played with him in the 1946/47 and 1948 series, similarly valued this and also having a second left hander in addition to Arthur Morris in his line-up.

By comparison, Barrington receives less credit from cricket writers for his steady, efficient run accumulation. He scored 50 or more in 46% of his innings against Australia, a figure only bettered by Bradman at 49% and Herbert Sutcliffe at 52%. At least CMJ puts Barrington in his top 50, describing him thus: "Craggy-jawed, crinkly haired, beaky nosed, brawny armed, dark-eyed and defiant, Ken Barrington was frequently England's rock during a life devoted to cricket".

The dominance of batsmen against bowlers between the wars, that we saw in Era 2, swung the other way in the 1950s and early-1960s due in part to rule changes. First there was the change to the LBW law, introduced experimentally in 1935 and then permanently in 1937, under which a batsman could be out to a ball pitching outside the off stump. Secondly, the no ball rule was changed in 1947 to allow the bowler to drag his back foot across the bowling crease during delivery, provided the foot initially landed behind the crease. This could make a difference of a yard or so for a fast bowler. It's notable that of the four Era 2 bowlers who achieved the qualifying condition of 75 wickets only one — Maurice Tate — was a fast bowler. Of the ten bowlers from Era 3 who qualified, eight were fast bowlers as were a further three of the four whose careers straddled Eras 3 and 4.

By the late 1950s, not only were the average runs per wicket declining but, as described above, so were scoring rates, quite alarmingly so. Cricket's leaders were concerned and sought to bring back more positivity to the game and to reverse its declining popularity which was particularly acute in England where football was by far the more popular game with school children. In 1957 the rule prohibiting more than two fielders behind the wicket on the leg side was introduced and in 1963 the front-foot no-ball rule was introduced (initially experimentally, but permanently from 1969) replacing the back-foot dragging rule to redress the balance which had swung too far against batsmen.

The pressure for more attractive cricket also spawned the one-day limited overs game. In England the Gillette Cup was introduced in 1963 (initially with 65 overs but soon reduced to 60) followed by the 40-over John Player League in 1969. As the amount of one-day cricket increased, the more positive attitude it required filtered through to the longer, first class games. From 1971 one day games also became part of the international calendar and by mid-1999 the cumulative total number of one day internationals played exceeded that of Test matches.

The influence of the West Indies was also considerable. Their tour of Australia in 1960/61 and the informal agreement between captains Richie Benaud and Frank Worrell to ensure attacking cricket was played, led to the first tied Test match, at Brisbane, and was a watershed for Test cricket even though its effects were hard to see in the Ashes tests of the early 1960s.

Hutton and Compton were certainly the mainstays of England's batting in the immediate post-War years. Their test careers ran very much in parallel, both beginning with the home series against New Zealand in 1937 and ending within a year or so of each other in the mid-1950s. Hutton played 27 Ashes tests and Compton 28. Hutton's Ashes raw average at 56.46 was very close to his overall Test average of 56.67. However, at 42.83, Compton's Ashes average was much lower than his overall test average of 50.06.

Both of them had excellent technique; it is said that when Hutton first came to the Yorkshire County nets as a young man that George Hirst the Yorkshire coach commented that there was nothing the county coaches could teach him. However, the two men had very different personalities; Hutton was serious and perhaps a little dour, Compton adventurous and flamboyant.

In six Ashes series Hutton's raw average fell below 50 only twice. He made five centuries against Australia. His first came in his Ashes debut at Trent Bridge in 1938, where he scored exactly 100. His second came at the Oval in the same series and was the record-breaking individual score of 364 which still stands as the highest in Ashes Tests. Hutton's other centuries were: 122 at Sydney in 1946/47, when he had to retire at 237-6 with tonsillitis and England totalled only 280, 156 not out at Adelaide in 1950/51, when he batted throughout the England innings of 272, and 145 at Lord's in 1953 an innings rated by some as his best.

Others rate his 62 not out at Brisbane in the first Test of the 1950/51 series as his best innings. Both England in their first innings and Australia in their second had been caught on an impossible sticky wicket, England declaring at 68-7 and then Australia at 32-7 both in an effort to catch the other side in the difficult conditions. England were set 193 to win and Hutton made 62 not out in an England losing total of 122. Although he couldn't save the game, Hutton seemed little troubled by a wicket that no one else seemed to be able to cope with. When needed, he played defensively with soft hands to drop the ball dead at his feet away from the close in-fielders and yet he was also able to play many beautiful drives through the offside.

Like Hutton, Compton also scored five centuries against Australia, and like Hutton he scored his first in his debut Ashes Test at Trent Bridge in 1938. Compton made two centuries in the match at Adelaide in 1946/47 helping England secure one of their two draws in a series they lost 3-0. In Bradman's last series in 1948 England lost again, this time 4-0. Compton's 184 at Trent Bridge couldn't save the game for England but his 145 at Manchester secured a draw and was widely considered his finest Ashes innings. England were batting first and Lindwall, at this time aided by the 1947 change in the no ball rule and liberal use of bouncers, was unmercifully hostile. In an era when there were no helmets, Compton was hit on his forehead just above his eye when he top edged an attempted hook off a Lindwall no ball. Blood poured from the cut and he had to retire. An indication of how hard the batsmen were having to battle in the conditions is that while Compton was off the field having stitches, the second new ball was taken with the score at just 87 for 2. This was under an experimental rule allowing a new ball after 55 overs. Compton returned to the crease at 119 for 5 after a middle order collapse and immediately showed confidence against Lindwall, batting on undefeated to 145 to lead England through to a first innings total of 363. England had already lost the first two Tests by the large margins of eight wickets and 409 runs and anything less from Compton could have left England open to going three down after only three games.

Interestingly both Hutton and Compton were handicapped by chronic injuries; Hutton's left arm was about 2 inches shorter than his right due to a war-time accident in the gym and Compton who played league football for Arsenal and in several war-time internationals, had a damaged knee from a football injury which increasingly restricted him later in his test cricket career.

3RD ERA BOWLERS

As with the batsmen there are upward and downward movements in the rankings from the adjustments.

It's worth remembering that although the adjusted average mechanism deals with the different balance between batsmen and bowlers in the different eras (and different matches) the circumstances of the time determined what types of bowling were popular and successful in any given era. As outlined above, the 1947 change to the no ball rule favoured pace bowlers and we have eight of these featured in this era. The 1937 LBW law favoured off spinners and a true off spinner, Jim Laker, is included for the first time since Hugh Trumble, Joey Palmer and George Giffen in era 1. Laker also finishes top of the adjusted rankings. While three of the four second era bowlers were leg spinners, the two rule changes did not favour that style of bowling and so Richie Benaud is the only featured third era leg spinner. He fares less well in the adjusted rankings than O'Reilly, Grimmett and Mailey from the previous era, which hints at the increasing relative advantage that the rule changes afforded both pace bowlers and off spinners.

3RD ERA BOWLERS

The results for the era 3 bowlers are:

	⚑	M	W	RAW AV	ADJ AV	RAW RK	ADJ RK
LINDWALL	AUS	29	114	22.44	24.02	14	10
BEDSER	ENG	21	104	27.49	26.82	30	26
MCKENZIE	AUS	25	96	31.34	28.57	38	36
MILLER	AUS	29	87	22.40	24.20	13	12
DAVIDSON	AUS	25	84	23.76	24.97	16	16
SNOW	ENG	20	83	25.61	24.40	24	13
BENAUD	AUS	27	83	31.81	32.98	39	42
LAKER	ENG	15	79	18.27	19.79	4	1
TRUEMAN	ENG	19	79	25.30	26.52	22	24
JOHNSTON	AUS	17	75	24.24	25.94	19	21

Of Laker's 79 wickets, 46 were taken in his record-breaking series in England in 1956, including the incredible 19 for 90 at Manchester. No-one else has even reached 40 wickets in a five-match series. In assessing Laker's achievement, we should remember of course that the pitches in 1956 suited him. But we should remember also that Australia had an off spinner of their own in Ian Johnson and that there were other spinners playing, in particular Tony Lock for England and Benaud for Australia, who could benefit from turning pitches even if the easy pace was rather less favourable to Benaud's leg spin. The average adjustment mechanism compensates for the lower runs per wicket in the matches during this series and it should also be remembered that Laker bowled in 15 matches and 28 innings, so his results reflect far more than just that one series. All the critics agree that he span the ball tremendously and Geoff Boycott has said that of all the bowlers he faced, only Laker made the ball hum audibly through the air.

The other bowler from this era who makes the adjusted top 10 is Ray Lindwall at tenth position with Keith Miller, who usually opened the bowling with him, just outside at 12th position. They broke onto the scene immediately after the war in the 1946/47 series, when Lindwall was already 24 and Miller 27, and were soon recognised as the fastest and most effective Australian opening attack since Jack Gregory and Ted McDonald.

Lindwall, with a beautifully smooth and fluid run up and delivery had modelled himself on Harold Larwood. Many critics felt he was as fast as Larwood and his relatively low action caused his bumpers to skid through dangerously at high chest- or throat-level. His control of pace, length and swing was legendary, and Len Hutton rated him first among the bowlers he faced. Admittedly Lindwall was helped by the 1947 no ball rule and in England in 1948 by the experimental law which allowed a second new ball to be taken after just 55 overs. He was equally as effective in Australia, where he took 54 wickets in 15 matches, and England where he took 60 wickets in 14 Tests. Bradman rated Lindwall's 6/20 in England's first innings at the Oval in 1948, which saw the hosts dismissed for just 52, as his finest bowling ever.

Lindwall and Miller both played 29 tests, 26 together, although rarely did they both succeed in the same innings. Bill Johnston, with more than 75 Ashes wickets, provided excellent support. Miller was a larger-than-life character, who was only happy if the cricket was truly competitive; once when the Australian batsmen were thrashing Essex in 1948, he went in to bat and deliberately allowed himself to be bowled for a duck. His cavalier approach to the game had its roots in his war-time experiences as a fighter pilot with the RAF. Having lost friends in combat and fought the Luftwaffe he didn't feel any pressure playing Test cricket. A back injury sustained during the war meant he was sometimes unable to bowl; however for most of his career he was well worth his place in the Test side as a batsman and Bill Johnston was quite able to take the new ball if required to do so. Miller's fun-loving attitude to life and to cricket did not always go down well with the authorities and this was almost certainly the reason he was overlooked for the captaincy on his last tour to England in 1956.

While Miller was not as consistently fast as Lindwall, his fastest deliveries were just as quick and he was unpredictable. A searing bouncer delivered from his high action might be followed by a yorker or by a leg break. His best bowling was against top class batsmen and most of his wickets were taken against them rather than those in the lower order. He took 7 for 60 on a difficult Brisbane wicket in his first Ashes Test, the first match after the war, to help Australia to their biggest ever win against England. Perhaps his best bowling performance was at Lord's in 1956 when, aged 37, he took 10 for 152 with five wickets in each innings. The performance gave Australia victory on what proved to be the only lasting hard true wicket of the series but couldn't prevent England winning the series.

At 13, John Snow is the highest ranked English pace bowler from this era. In the late 1960s Snow was the pre-eminent fast bowler in Ashes Tests. His 31 wickets in the six-match 1970/71 series were the foundation from which Ray Illingworth's team were able to reclaim the Ashes. Genuinely fast yet without the benefit of the back-foot draggers rule (the front-foot no ball rule had come into force in 1963), he was quick enough to worry even the top batsmen with bouncers. Trueman had a better raw average than Snow but played in lower scoring Test matches so drops to 24 in the adjusted rankings. Better known because of his fiery character and more often included in all-time Test sides than Snow, Trueman played fewer Tests than he might have done in the 1950s. He began National Service in 1951 and was not demobilised until 1953, which curtailed his involvement in first class matches for two seasons, and he was not selected for the 1954/55 tour Down Under after a series of misdemeanours on the tour of the West Indies the previous winter.

At 16 and 21 in the adjusted rankings, left armers Alan Davidson and Bill Johnston delivered many strong performances but could not match the overall figures or charisma of their contemporaries, Lindwall and Miller. McKenzie, who features at 36 in the adjusted rankings, is the only featured Australian bowler who played between the end of Davidson's Ashes career in 1963 and the arrival of Lillee in the 1970/71 series.

Alec Bedser, who is 26th in the adjusted rankings, was a medium fast, rather than a genuinely fast, opening bowler with a leg cutter good enough to bowl Bradman on an easy Adelaide pitch in 1946/47. Bedser was rated highly by Bradman, who included him in his all-time England XI, and also by CMJ, who named him 29th in his top 100. This acknowledgement from his peers and the pundits may be because the burden of the opening attack against Australia in the immediate post-War years fell squarely on his shoulders. Notwithstanding support from Trevor Bailey it was not really until Trueman, Brian Statham and Frank Tyson arrived that he could pass the burden on.

Benaud at 42 in the rankings was a class leg-spinner and also a fine captain and late middle order batsman. However, the rule changes, primarily that to the LBW law, meant that leg-spinners were less favoured than other bowlers in his era and he could not really hope to challenge Grimmett, O'Reilly and Mailey in the rankings.

1977 TO 2000

By the time Australia won the Centenary Test, the wheels were already in motion for an independent project that would have an immediate and major impact on Ashes cricket. In fact, not only did Kerry Packer's World Series cricket (WSC) directly affect the Australian Test team during the two years of its existence, but it also affected the future scale of one day cricket after the tournament was discontinued.

The WSC arose because of the existence of two key factors: Kerry Packer's failed attempt to buy the TV rights for Australian Test matches and the relatively low pay of Australian cricketers. Packer, the owner of the Australia Nine Network, had tried to buy the rights to televise Australian home Tests, yet despite the fact his offer was higher, the Australian Cricket Board stuck with the State Australian Broadcasting Commission for the rights. Undeterred, Packer decided to arrange a series of exhibition games between an Australian side and the Rest of the World. The TV magnate was able to take advantage of the fact that Australian Test players were poorly remunerated and were not contracted to the Australian Cricket Board. Their livelihood depended on contracts with the state sides for Sheffield Shield cricket and on other careers. The amounts they were paid by the Australian Cricket Board for Tests were very small by the standards of other international sports stars. For example, it is said that each player received less than $3,000 for the 1975 tour of England meaning that on occasion some players were unable to go on tours simply because they could not afford it. Exploiting these low salaries and the players' resulting lack of loyalty to the Board, Packer signed up Australia's entire first team side apart from Jeff Thomson, who was prevented from playing in the WSC by his contract with a Brisbane radio station.

This meant that over the two year period before a compromise agreement was reached in 1979, Australia were without their top players who, having signed with WSC, were banned from playing international cricket. England lost Tony Greig, Dennis Amiss, Alan Knott, Bob Woolmer and Derek Underwood from those who had played in the 1977 series but the others, including Geoff Boycott, Mike Brearley, the seam bowlers Bob Willis, Chris Old and Mike Hendrick, and also Derek Randall and Graham Gooch, did not join WSC. With Ian Botham and David Gower, two of England's most exciting players for many years about to make their mark, England were in much better shape than their rivals.

The news of WSC broke on the eve of Australia's 1977 tour of England. Greig was sacked as captain, in favour of Mike Brearley, but he and the other English WSC players still played in the 1977 series, though not subsequently for England during the duration of the WSC. Australia, with vastly more players involved, were already in England with the tour party (except for Ian Chappell who had already made himself unavailable, because of his very close association with WSC, and Dennis Lillee who was injured). The news had a demoralising effect on the Australians and they lost the series 3-0. Unbelievably it was the first time England had won three matches in a home series since 1886. The third 1977 Test at Trent Bridge saw the return of Boycott and in three matches he scored 442 runs, at a raw average of 147.3 and an adjusted average of 156.6, both these average figures being records for an Ashes series. At his home ground at Headingley he completed his 100th first class 100 also becoming only the fourth England player to be on the field for an entire Test match.

The next series in 1978/79 in Australia gave England a 5-1 win. Australia, a shadow of themselves without the WSC players, had only Rodney Hogg to turn in a star performance with 41 wickets, still a record for Australia in Australia (albeit in a six-Test series). Hogg only played five more Ashes Tests and so with 56 wickets doesn't meet our 75-wicket qualification mark; however he is discussed in Chapter 8, where we look at players who just missed the cut.

The short three-match series in Australia in 1979/80 saw the return of the WSC players and a 3-0 victory for the hosts, and the single test at Lord's in 1980 to celebrate the centenary of the first Test played in England (though the original match was at the Oval) was a disappointing draw with the loss of much time to rain. Australia set England the target of scoring 370 to win in 350 minutes, a challenge the hosts did not take up, finishing on 244/3. Although the Ashes were not at stake in any of these games, the matches still constitute Test matches between England and Australia and are therefore included in compiling the relevant players' averages.

Botham led England in this Centenary Test, and he also led England in the first two Tests in 1981. However the captaincy was affecting his batting and bowling and he stepped down after the second of those games. With Brearley reinstated as skipper, Botham's form improved considerably. In the third Test at Headingley, he took 6-95 in Australia's first innings but this and his top score of 50 when England batted still couldn't prevent them being forced to follow on 227 runs behind. Botham now stepped up a gear with a swashbuckling second innings of 149 not out. This inspired England to dismiss Australia for just 111 in their second innings and record a sensational win by just 18 runs. This was the first time that a team which had followed on had gone on to win an Ashes Test since 1894. It was Bob Willis with dramatic bowling figures of 8-43 in Australia's second innings, who turned the opportunity created by Botham into a historic victory. Two more wins, helped in no small part by Botham's all-round performances gave England a 3-1 series win in what became known as Botham's Ashes.

England lost 2-1 in Australia in 1982/83 largely due to the bowling of Geoff Lawson, who was ably supported by Jeff Thomson. England regained the Ashes at home in 1985 thanks to a 3-1 victory in a series notable for Gower's aggregate of 732 runs, a record for an Englishman in England in an Ashes series. Having not won three matches in a home Ashes series for 90 years, England had now achieved it in three successive home series. The Ashes were retained in Australia in 1986/87 with a strong all-round performance.

However, the picture changed from 1989 as Australia, initially under the captaincy of Allan Border, began the domination of the Ashes which would not end until England eventually regained The Urn in 2005. Australia won eight consecutive Test series, including the last six of this era which ends with the final series of the 20th century, in Australia in 1998/99. In those six series, Australia notched up 20 test wins to England's five. England lost the first, six-match, series of this period, in 1989, 4-0. Taylor scored 839 runs, an Ashes series aggregate only bettered by Donald Bradman and Wally Hammond. Terry Alderman took 41 wickets and Steve Waugh, making his Ashes debut, recorded 393 runs before he was dismissed for the first time in the first innings of the third Test. It was Botham's final Ashes series, and David Gower would play his last in the following series in the winter of 1990/91. Their departures from the stage meant that England would struggle to compete either with the batting of Border, Waugh and Waugh's twin brother, Mark, or the pace bowling of Lawson, Terry Alderman, Merv Hughes and Craig McDermott over the coming years.

The series in Australia in 1990/91 saw a debut century by Mark Waugh and a victory for Australia by 3-0 largely due to the pace bowling of Alderman, McDermott and Bruce Reid who took 60 wickets between them. Graham Gooch, who was England captain for this series, missed the first Test, which Australia won by 10 wickets, through injury. He returned with a half century in the second Test but couldn't prevent defeat by eight wickets. Another 50 in the third Test helped England to a draw and in the second innings of the fourth he put on 203 for the first wicket along with Mike Atherton. Their stand briefly made the unlikely looking target of 472 look achievable before a middle order collapse led to a draw. Australia ran out winners of the final Test by nine wickets.

Australia's tour to England in 1993 was memorable for Shane Warne's 'Ball of the Century'. With his very first delivery, the spinner bowled Mike Gatting with a leg break which pitched well outside leg and took the top of off stump. It seemed to set the tone for the series, Australia winning 4-1 including two victories by an innings, another by 8 wickets and a fourth by 179 runs. After Australia won the fourth Test to clinch the Ashes, with Allan Border and Steve Waugh making an unbroken fifth wicket partnership of 332, Gooch resigned as captain and Atherton took over for the remaining two matches.

Glenn McGrath made his Ashes debut in 1994/95 but played in only two Tests. Australia continued their winning streak with a series win of 3-1 thanks to the bowling of Warne and McDermott and a series aggregate of over 600 runs from Michael Slater.

England started the 1997 series positively thanks to a double hundred from Nasser Hussain and strong pace bowling from Andy Caddick and Darren Gough. The rain-affected second Test was drawn. The bowling of McGrath and Warne and strong all-round batting powered Australia to victory in the next three Tests, and the series. England wrapped up proceedings with victory in the final Test at The Oval.

Warne was unavailable until the final test of the 1998/99 series because of a shoulder injury. In his absence, leg spinner Stuart MacGill came into the side and took 27 wickets. Slater made three hundreds and Justin Langer chipped in with 179 at Adelaide. This powerful batting plus the bowling of MacGill and McGrath was too much for England, who had insufficient strength or depth in either department to compete seriously and lost the series by 3-1.

As with Era 3 the average batting runs per wicket in the 4th Era, this time 29.5, are close to the overall average of 28.9. Therefore, but for the odd exception, the changes from the raw rankings to the adjusted rankings among the batsmen are not vast. Twelve of the 61 batsmen who meet our criteria are from this era, with a further four straddling eras 3 and 4. Conversely, among the bowlers, although the difference between the era average runs conceded per wicket taken of 30.8 and the overall average of 30.1 is much the same as for the batsmen there is more volatility and change from raw rankings to the adjusted rankings. Six of the 43 featured bowlers are from this era with a further four straddling eras 3 and 4 and another two straddling eras 4 and 5.

4TH ERA BATSMEN

The results for Era 4 batsmen are as follows:

		M	R	RAW AV	ADJ AV	RAW RK	ADJ RK
BORDER	AUS	47	3548	56.31	51.01	8	8
GOWER	ENG	42	3269	44.78	43.88	24	18
S WAUGH	AUS	46	3200	58.18	53.75	5	6
GOOCH	ENG	42	2632	33.31	31.07	49	57
M TAYLOR	AUS	33	2496	42.30	38.76	29	29
BOON	AUS	31	2237	45.65	37.47	21	34
M WAUGH	AUS	29	2204	50.09	49.27	13	11
ATHERTON	ENG	33	1900	29.68	27.62	58	60
A STEWART	ENG	33	1810	30.67	29.84	57	58
BOTHAM	ENG	36	1673	29.35	32.00	59	55
SLATER	AUS	20	1669	45.10	42.94	22	19
GATTING	ENG	27	1661	37.75	34.01	40	45

Two batsmen from this era, Steve Waugh and Allan Border, make our overall top ten at numbers six and eight respectively. Border played 47 Ashes tests and Steve Waugh 46 and both scored considerably more than 3,000 runs in Tests against England. Their careers overlapped between 1986 and 1993 when they played 19 Tests together against England with Border as captain.

Both were tough characters in the traditional Australian mould and there is some parallel in their batting records. As middle-order batsmen with strong discipline they rarely gave their wickets away easily and were left 'not out' more than most. Border had 19 not outs in his 82 innings and Steve Waugh 18 in his 73 innings. On the five occasions when Steve Waugh reached 120, he never got out. Border had five not outs in his eight Ashes centuries. At Headingley in 1993 they both achieved this in the same innings when they came together at 321-4 and put on 332 in an unbroken stand before Border declared at 653-4 with himself on 200 not out and Steve Waugh on 157 not out. It remains the highest total at

Headingley and Australia's highest fifth wicket partnership against England in England.

Their entries on to the Test scene were different. Border was selected earlier than he might otherwise have been, in 1978/79, because of the mass departure of Australia's first choice XI to Kerry Packer's WSC. In 1984 he became a reluctant captain when Kim Hughes dramatically resigned. England were strongly in the ascendancy at the time but after their victories in the series of 1985 and 1986/87 the position reversed and Border led Australia to victory in three Ashes series. Mark Taylor then did likewise before Steve Waugh took over the captaincy to win the first two series of the next era in 2001 and 2002/03.

Steve Waugh came upon the scene in 1986/87 as a batsman of whom there were high expectations and he had a pivotal role in Australia regaining the Ashes in 1989 making 350 runs in the first two Tests without being dismissed to take Australia to a 2-0 lead. It is also notable that both Border and Waugh had significantly higher raw averages against England than they did in tests generally.

However, neither Border nor Waugh feature in Bradman's all time Australian Ashes team nor in Boycott's all-time Australian team, both of them preferring Neil Harvey, who represented Australia in Era 3. Boycott also includes Greg Chappell, whose raw average for Tests overall is in fact a little ahead of Border's and Waugh's, although his Ashes average is much lower. CMJ ranks Chappell at 38, ahead of Border and Waugh (55 and 63 respectively) but he places Harvey behind both.

At position 11 in the adjusted rankings is Steve Waugh's twin brother Mark who played 29 matches adding weight to the batting in Australia's dominant side during the 1990s. England's highest batsman from this era, David Gower comes in at 18th with an adjusted average of 43.88. This is more than five runs per innings behind Mark Waugh and more than seven runs per innings behind Allan Border. Yet Gower is nearly 10 runs per innings and 25 places in the rankings higher than Mike Gatting, who is next among the English batsmen from the era. This serves to underline the Australian dominance of the 1990s.

The other featured Australian batsmen, Taylor and David Boon are 11 and 16 places respectively behind Gower but are still comfortably above the rest of England's batsmen namely Gatting, Botham, Gooch,

Alec Stewart and Atherton. Of course, one mustn't just evaluate Botham as a batsman but as an all-rounder who is one of four players who have achieved the qualification conditions for both batting and bowling, the others being Wilfred Rhodes, Monty Noble and Keith Miller (and we do this evaluation in Chapter 9).

To return to Gower, despite his comparatively modest ranking of 18 and the general agreement of the critics that he would not be included in an all-time England Ashes side, he has several claims to fame. Only Hobbs has scored more centuries against Australia than Gower's nine (Hammond also had nine) and Gower holds the record aggregate of 732 for an English batsman in a series against Australia in England. Furthermore, in the opinion of no lesser mortal than Don Bradman himself, Gower played the finest innings in Australia in an Ashes test (by either an Australian or an Englishman) that Bradman ever saw. This was Gower's 123 in the third Test at Sydney in the 1990/91 series.

4TH ERA BOWLERS

Five of the six bowlers who played primarily in Era 4 and three of the additional four bowlers whose careers were split between this and another era were seam bowlers. Other than Botham and Emburey and to a lesser extent, Alderman, these Era 4 bowlers played more in the games in the era when runs per wicket were higher, which accordingly leads to the adjustment mechanism lowering their averages. The figures are as follows:

	⚐	M	W	RAW AV	ADJ AV	RAW RK	ADJ RK
BOTHAM	ENG	36	148	27.65	28.37	31	34
ALDERMAN	AUS	17	100	21.17	22.15	10	4
LAWSON	AUS	21	97	28.48	24.56	32	14
MCDERMOTT	AUS	17	84	26.31	23.04	27	6
EMBUREY	ENG	25	78	34.59	31.85	43	41
M HUGHES	AUS	20	75	30.25	26.25	35	22

Alderman leads the bowlers of this era and only Jim Laker, Glenn McGrath and Shane Warne outstrip him in the overall rankings. He is also the only bowler to have taken more than 40 wickets in a series on two separate occasions and has the highest strike rate per match of any bowler other than Charlie Turner and Tom Richardson who played in the first era, and thus in very different conditions.

Alderman made his debut in the first Test of the 1981 series and took 42 wickets in that series (the record for an Australian in England, albeit in a six-match series). Early in the first match of the next series in Australia in 1982/83 he dislocated his shoulder in bizarre circumstances as he brought down a pitch invader with a rugby tackle and he subsequently missed the rest of the series. He then missed the next two series because of involvement with a rebel South African tour and didn't play against England again until the 1989 series when he took 41 wickets at little more than 16 apiece, helping Australia to a 4-0 series win beginning their long dominance over England, which lasted until 2005. The English conditions suited Alderman's accuracy, pace variation and full-length away swing. He was nowhere near as successful in Australian conditions nor in Tests against other countries.

McDermott, who was genuinely fast, also took most of his wickets against England in two series that were many years apart. He took 30 wickets in his debut series against England in 1985, aged just 20 but inconsistent form and injuries meant that he only played in six of the next 17 Tests against England before playing in all five matches in 1994/5 and taking 32 wickets. With Lawson and Hughes also performing strongly, pace bowling continued to dominate the Australian attack.

This leaves the two English bowlers in this era Botham and John Emburey. As with his batting, Botham's bowling must be judged in the context of his all-round performances. Emburey had some good performances including five wickets in the second innings of both the first match in the 1985 series and the first match of the 1986/87 series helping England to take a 1-0 lead and setting up series wins in both cases. However, he wasn't as consistently successful as would be needed to feature highly in the rankings.

BATSMEN ERAS 3/4

There are four featured batsmen whose careers
straddled Eras 3 and 4. These are:

	⚑	M	R	RAW AV	ADJ AV	RAW RK	ADJ RK
BOYCOTT	ENG	38	2945	47.50	46.28	17	14
G CHAPPELL	AUS	35	2619	45.94	44.91	20	16
KNOTT	ENG	34	1682	32.98	32.20	51	53
R MARSH	AUS	42	1633	27.21	28.33	60	59

Boycott was an opening batsman in the true Yorkshire mould. Always
in control of his play throughout his career from 1963 to 1981, he
was generally the first choice England opening batsman except for
his three-year self-imposed hiatus between 1974 and 1977 and only
Gower and Hobbs have scored more runs against Australia. As
mentioned above Boycott reached his 100th first class hundred at
Headingley against Australia. It seemed just reward for the many
times when he remained at the crease playing technically correct
strokes in difficult conditions when others were failing through lack
of ability or, inexcusably in his opinion, through lack of concentration
and application. A number of his innings showed the wide range of
strokes which he could play; however he would always restrict himself
to those he thought safe to play in the prevailing conditions.

One statistic which underlines his value to England is the success
percentage in the games in which he played. With a figure of 55%
he is surpassed by only seven of the other 42 core England players
featured in this book only three of whom played after era 1. Another
interesting statistic about him, although it relates to raw averages in
first class cricket rather than adjusted averages in Ashes Tests, is that
Boycott has the highest average of the 62 batsmen who have reached
30,000 first class runs, yet further testament to the discipline he
imposed on himself.

Greg Chappell, one of three brothers who played cricket for
Australia, comes in at 16 and his skill earned him a place in Geoff

Boycott's all time Australian squad. His record against England was less strong than his overall record but he was the leading Australian batsman of his time and his tally of nine centuries against England is only surpassed by Steve Waugh's 10 and Don Bradman's 19.

Alan Knott and Rod Marsh are the only wicket keepers other than Alec Stewart to qualify for the batting rankings (in fact Stewart did not keep wicket in all the Tests he played against Australia and would not meet the batting qualification if his runs in matches when he did not keep wicket were excluded). At 53 Knott is above three modern day England opening batsmen (one of whom is Stewart) and also above the legendary Frank Woolley.

BOWLERS ERAS 3/4

Similarly, there are four bowlers who feature in both Era 3 and 4:

	⚑	M	W	RAW AV	ADJ AV	RAW RK	ADJ RK
LILLEE	AUS	29	167	21.00	22.41	9	5
WILLIS	ENG	35	128	26.14	28.96	26	38
UNDERWOOD	ENG	29	105	26.38	26.39	28	23
THOMSON	AUS	21	100	24.18	24.09	18	11

Lillee's career spanned 1970 to 1983 and his tally of 167 wickets is the highest of any pace bowler and second overall only to Warne. Lillee, who ranks fifth in our overall list, took 20 wickets in an Ashes series no fewer than five times and took 11 wickets in the historic Centenary Test in 1977. Jeff Thomson, his opening partner in the 1974/75 and 1975 series which Australia won in large part due to the ferocity of their attack, is just outside the top ten at 11th.

Derek Underwood, who bowled his left arm spin more quickly and with a flatter trajectory than the classic orthodox left arm slows, was thought of as being more effective on English wickets. However, he nevertheless took 50 of his 105 wickets in Australia. Despite a ranking of 38, Bob Willis is second only to Botham in tally of wickets for England against Australia. His eight for 43 turned Botham's incredible all round performances in the 3rd test in 1981 into a win by 18 runs, bookmakers having quoted odds against England of 500-1 less than 48 hours earlier.

2001 TO 2019

The new century began in a familiar pattern with Australia, led by Steve Waugh, beating Nasser Hussain's England, in both of the first two Test series, by the same 4-1 scoreline. Of the two games England did win, one was against an Australian side captained by Adam Gilchrist in Waugh's absence. At Headingley, in August 2001, Gilchrist declared on 176/4 to set England 315 to win in 110 overs. Mark Butcher played a superb innings of 173 not out to see the hosts home with 20 overs to spare. It was a small dent in the continuing Australian dominance and remains one of only two occasions in Ashes history when a side has successfully chased a target set by a declaration, the other also being at Leeds 53 years earlier when Australia successfully reached their target of 404, to win by seven wickets. Australia's eight victories in these first two series after the turn of the century were all by comfortable margins, four of them by an innings.

By the time the 2005 series started England, under Michael Vaughan, felt more confident, having won their previous four Test series (against West Indies twice, New Zealand and South Africa). Initially it looked as if events might follow the path of previous Ashes series after England lost the first Test by 239 runs. However, Australia lost Glenn McGrath on the morning of the second Test to injury in practice and, after having been put in, Vaughan's side reached 407 by the end of the first day. Despite being bowled out for 182 in the second innings, England set Australia 282 to win. In a thrilling finish that saw Australia move from 137-7 to the brink of victory at 279-9, England took the last wicket to win by just 2 runs, the closest result in Ashes history. The third Test was another nail-biter which saw Australia's 10th wicket partnership of McGrath and Brett Lee see out the final four overs to hold on for a draw. England took the fourth Test at Trent Bridge by three wickets meaning that the draw they subsequently secured in the final Test was enough to give them the Ashes for the first time since they lost them to Allan Border's side 16 years previously.

It didn't take long for Australia to gain their revenge, something they did in emphatic style. They needed just three matches of the 2006/07 series to move into an unassailable 3-0 lead. They then went on to win the final two games to seal the first Ashes whitewash since England lost 5-0 in Australia in 1920/21 in the first series after the First World War. While Andrew Flintoff, captaining England in Vaughan's absence, made mistakes, the most notable being at Adelaide when he declared at 551-6 in the first innings only for England to lose by six wickets when they collapsed in the second, Australia were much too strong for England. It had been thought that both Warne and McGrath might retire after the 2005 series but, perhaps seeking the opportunity to go out with a series victory, they stayed on for 2006/07. Their contributions were significant, with Warne taking 23 wickets in the series and McGrath taking 21. In the process, they cemented their places as the highest and third highest wicket takers in Ashes history. Adam Gilchrist, Justin Langer and Mathew Hayden would all also retire before the next Ashes series.

So, by 2009, other than captain Ricky Ponting, the Australian team looked very different. Andrew Strauss had been installed as England captain and after four Tests it was all square at one apiece. England narrowly avoided defeat to claim a draw at Cardiff, before posting their first win against Australia at Lord's since 1934, by 115 runs. The third Test at Edgbaston was a draw and Australia won by an innings and 80 runs at Headingley. At the Oval the bowling of Graeme Swann and Stuart Broad gave England a first innings lead of 172 which proved decisive and the Ashes were back in England.

England travelled to Australia in 2010/11 with Strauss continuing as captain and Alastair Cook accumulating 766 runs in the series including his maiden Test double century. By contrast, the home side were without their iconic players of 2006/07 and their two leading batsmen, Ponting and Michael Clarke, had dismal series averaging

16 and 21 respectively. Strong team performances in all the games except at Perth, gave England a series win of 3-1 which meant Strauss joined Mike Brearley and Len Hutton as the only England captains to win victories in Ashes series both home and away.

The Australian touring team of 2013 was said by some to be the weakest ever to come to England. Only Clarke had a solid reputation as a batsman and of the bowlers Mitchell Johnson, the leading wicket taker, was left out, leaving the burden on Peter Siddle, Ryan Harris and several relative newcomers of whom only pace bowler Mitchell Starc and spinner Nathan Lyon played as many as three Tests each. Some rash English commentators predicted a whitewash.

By the end of the series Australia had lost 3-0 but the gap between the two sides had not been as great as expected. In the first Test at Nottingham, Australia gave England a shock, dismissing them for just 215 in the first innings before scoring 280 themselves, thanks to a last-wicket partnership of 163 (which included 98 at number 11 by debutant Ashton Agar). Ultimately set 311 for victory, the tourists fell short by just 14 runs. It was Jimmy Anderson's ten wickets and Ian Bell's second innings century which saw England through.

At Lord's, another century from Bell, 180 from Joe Root and nine wickets from Swann saw England through to a strong 347 run victory. However Australia would almost certainly have won at Manchester had it not been for the weather, and in the final test at the Oval, the tourists were arguably again robbed by the weather, though in attempting to force a win with an adventurous declaration, Clarke nearly handed victory to England. Sandwiched between these two drawn games was the first ever Ashes Test played at the Riverside in Chester-le-Street. This was closely fought but ultimately 11 for 121 from Broad and a third series hundred from Bell trumped a century from Chris Rogers and nine wickets from Harris to see England home by 74 runs.

The 2013 series was immediately followed by the 2013/14 series in Australia, the first case of back-to-back series since 1974/75 and 1975. England started as favourites but this soon proved to be a wholly misplaced prediction. The series was characterised by the triumphant return of Mitchell Johnson, a continuation of Ryan Harris's fine bowling in England during the summer, a record series run aggregate for a wicketkeeper by Brad Haddin and repeated batting failures by England. No England batsman managed as many as 300 runs in the series and the only century came from debutant all-rounder Ben Stokes, who also turned in one of England's best bowling performances with six for 99 at Sydney. England could not deal with the pace of Johnson, who took 37 wickets in the series at just 14 runs apiece, and Harris, who took 22 wickets at 19 apiece.

On the occasions when England seemed to have a slight advantage (which happened in Brisbane, Perth, Melbourne and Sydney) Haddin's batting would come to the rescue or England would catastrophically collapse as they did twice in the second innings at Melbourne from 86 for 1 to 87 for 4 and again from 173 for 5 to 179 all out. Australia won the series 5-0 and no-one could say it was not fully deserved. The pressures on England manifested themselves not only in the poor performances but also in high levels of stress on Jonathan Trott who had to leave the tour after the first Test and in the decision of Graeme Swann to retire from Test cricket and immediately return to England after the third Test. England were left to lick their wounds and to consider how to rebuild the side before the next series in England in 2015.

Rebuild they certainly did with a result more impressive than was expected by most pundits at the start of the series. Andrew Strauss, England's victorious captain in 2009 and 2010/11, took over from Paul Downton as director of cricket. He replaced the head coach Peter Moores with Trevor Bayliss, an Australian, and made it clear that Kevin Pietersen would not be returning to the side, bringing to an end widespread speculation about Pietersen's future which had continued ever since he had been dropped by England after the 2013/14 series in Australia. Pietersen certainly polarised opinion. Whilst many thought he was the best batsman England had, and should automatically play, an equal number considered him to have a negative impact on the team.

From Australia's victorious 2013/14 team Harris had been forced to retire through recurrent injury but Johnson was there and so was Mitchell Starc. The pundits generally thought that Australia were the stronger side and that England were at a low ebb having had a disastrous one-day World Cup in Australia before only drawing their series in the

West Indies a few months earlier (in contrast Australia had beaten the West Indies convincingly shortly after England's visit). The reality was different. Although England's initial victory at Cardiff, largely due to superior batting led by Joe Root, was swiftly negated by a crushing Australian victory at Lord's, where Steve Smith's double century led Australia to a total of 566-8 declared, the tide turned conclusively in England's favour during the third Test at Edgbaston. Anderson's six wickets wrecked Australia's first innings and they never sufficiently recovered allowing England to take victory by eight wickets.

In the fourth Test at Trent Bridge, Broad led the bowling attack so effectively in Anderson's absence that Australia were dismissed for 60 before lunch in just 18.3 overs. In the process, Broad recorded the third best ever Ashes bowling figures of 8-15 (the top two performances of 9-37 and 10-53 were both by Jim Laker in the same match at Manchester in 1956). England were helped by the Australian batsmen's determination to play aggressive cricket despite the conditions favouring the bowlers and by their apparent refusal to show the application necessary. Eight of the ten first innings wickets fell to slip catches. This is the shortest ever innings in Ashes history, though not of course by any means the lowest score, and the game only lasted until the third day. England won by an innings to retake the Ashes 3-1 with one match to play. Australian captain, Michael Clarke, at 34 a veteran of seven Ashes series, did not enjoy a good time with the bat, and given the criticism he received, few were surprised when he announced after Trent Bridge that he would retire from Test cricket at the end of the series.

However, anyone who thought England had a chance at the Oval to record an unprecedented fourth victory in a home Ashes series was soon disappointed. England's decision to put Australia in to bat, criticised by some with experience of the Oval wicket, did not bear fruit. Not only did Australia show they had learnt from Trent Bridge that patient application was sometimes the order of the day, the conditions did not favour England's seam bowlers in the same way as at Cardiff, Edgbaston and Trent Bridge. In reply to Australia's 481 England showed that they too could play injudicious shots and no one managed more than 30 as the home side were skittled for 149. Following on they fared a little better, but were all out for 286, thus

losing by an innings and 46 runs to end a series in which no match
was as closely fought as the 3-2 result might have suggested.

Following the disastrous showing by England in Australia in
2013/14 the pundits were cautious in their opinions on England's
prospects for 2017/18. Whatever England's chances might have been
they fell considerably when star all-rounder Ben Stokes was dropped
from the tour party after an incident outside a night club which led to
him being charged with affray. (Stokes was recalled to the Test side
after the Ashes series and played seven of the next nine matches in
2018. He was acquitted of the charge of affray at his trial in August
2018 and although he pleaded guilty to a charge of bringing the game
into disrepute in December 2018 the ban which was imposed by the
Cricket Disciplinary Commission was retroactive and had already
been served leaving Stokes able to resume his Test career in 2019).
Without Stokes in 2017/18 England failed to provide competitive
opposition for Australia though they battled much better than in
2013/14. England's bowlers lacked the pace of the Australian trio
of Starc, Cummins and Hazlewood all of whom took more wickets
at a lower raw average than Anderson, who was far and away the
best of the England bowlers. Nathan Lyon, the Australian off spin
bowler also took more wickets than any of the England bowlers
causing particular problems for the England left-handers. Moeen
Ali, the only specialist England spinner until the last test at Sydney
when Mason Crane made his debut as a leg spinner, was ineffective
with just five wickets at an average of 115.

Among the batsmen Dawid Malan with a raw series average of
42.69 was the most successful of the three relative newcomers with
both Vince and Stoneman averaging only in the twenties. Alastair
Cook and Joe Root both disappointed; Root made five fifties but did
not convert a single one to a century and Cook only passed 50 once
though he then batted through the innings to finish not out on 244.
This was only the fourteenth double century made by an Englishman
against Australia and the second by Cook making him the only
batsman other than Hammond to score more than one.

Steve Smith was the outstanding batsman for Australia making
centuries in three tests all at times when England might otherwise
have been strongly placed. His 239 at Perth was his second double

century against England and Australia's twenty fifth. He finished the series with 687 runs at a raw average of 137.4. There were six other centuries by Australians.

The result of all this was a 4-0 series win for Australia with England saving the game only at Melbourne where Mitchell Starc was injured and unable to play and Cook made his 244 not out. Two of the wins were by an innings, one by ten wickets and the other at Adelaide by 120 runs. England's best hopes were thought to have been at Adelaide, a day/night match (play was from 2pm to 9pm) where conditions were expected to favour seam movement and swing more than at the other four matches. Root won the toss and put Australia in to bat but England's pace bowling was too short and Australia amassed 442 for 8 declared. Better length bowling from Australia and four wickets for off spinner Nathan Lyon dismissed England for 227 and despite a much better second innings bowling performance from England the chance had been lost. The last Test saw an Australian total of 649-7, which included centuries from each of the Marsh brothers, both centuries being completed during a stand between the two brothers of 169, leading to Australia's second win of the series by an innings. England's supporters were left hoping not only that the Ashes could be regained in England in 2019 but also that England had learned enough about the need for real pace and real spin in Australia to ensure a team with the right combination of abilities would be sent for the next tour in 2021/22.

In March 2018 the notorious ball tampering incident occurred in South Africa where Australia were caught using sandpaper on the ball in an attempt to gain an illegitimate advantage from increased swing. This severely damaged the reputations of Smith and Warner and also Cameron Bancroft. Smith and Warner were banned from international cricket for a year and Bancroft for nine months. In addition, Smith and Bancroft were excluded from consideration for management roles for a further year and Warner excluded permanently. However, the timing of the bans meant that all three could return in time both for the 50 over ODI World Cup in England starting in May 2019 and for the Ashes series starting in August 2019, which they duly did, although Bancroft was dropped after the second Ashes match and Smith missed one match through injury.

England's World Cup triumph had cemented the reputations of Ben Stokes and a new young fast bowler Jofra Archer whose performance in the tournament had made him an automatic choice to join Anderson and Broad in the pace attack for the Ashes. In the event there were certain doubts over the full fitness of both Anderson and Archer for the first Test and, since it was considered unwise to risk both, Archer did not play in that first Test. It then transpired that Anderson was only able to bowl four overs and despite five wickets for Broad in the first innings helping England to a lead of 90, Australia were able to declare at 487 for 7 in their second knock and record a comfortable win by 251 runs with Smith, on his return to Test cricket, scoring 144 in the first innings and 142 in the second.

The second match at Lord's was drawn largely because of time lost to the weather but there was nonetheless plenty of excitement and some anxiety. On his debut, Archer showed not only that he had real pace and bounce but also that batsmen often could not identify the dangerous lifting balls in good time. Steve Smith, whose protective helmet did not include the additional recommended neck protector, was felled by a blow to the neck from one of these Archer deliveries prompting immediate concern. He was required by concussion procedure to retire hurt for an assessment which was clear and allowed him to return at the fall of the next wicket. Although he progressed his score to 92 before being dismissed, he did not look comfortable and a further assessment overnight showed symptoms of concussion which obliged him to withdraw from the remainder of the match. Under ICC concussion rules a substitute player, Marnus Labuschagne, was brought in and he became a full replacement for Smith, being permitted to bat and bowl as well as field. A fine not-out century by Ben Stokes gave England a chance of a win by enabling them to declare and set Australia a fourth innings target but despite the early loss of three wickets it became apparent that a result would not be achieved. Australia fell well short with six wickets down but were rarely in any real danger of losing thanks in no small part to a robust 59 from newcomer Labuschagne.

The third Test at Headingley was one of the most dramatic in Ashes history. Australia were without Smith, who needed more time than the short four-day interval after Lord's to recover fully from his concussion, and England should have been in the driving seat after Root put Australia in to bat and Archer took 6-45 to dismiss them for 179. However, England relinquished this position completely when superb Australian pace bowling from Hazlewood, Cummins and Pattinson dismissed them for 67, their lowest score against the Aussies since 1948. England's main strike bowler Archer might have expected to be used in short spells, but he had bowled more than anyone else in the first innings and his burden was compounded when Australia's second innings came around so soon. He needed relief and Ben Stokes came to the rescue, bowling half as many overs again as any of the other pace bowlers in Australia's second innings, taking three wickets and restricting the score to 246. Nevertheless, the target for England was 359, more than their most successful fourth innings run chase which had occurred 90 years previously at Melbourne when their first three batsmen had been Hobbs, Sutcliffe and Hammond. With well over two full days left for play few expected anything other than an Australian victory.

More than 200 runs were needed when Stokes came in at the fall of the third wicket and 74 were still required when the ninth wicket fell. Number 11, Jack Leach, with previous batting success as night watchman in England's first Test match against Ireland earlier in the summer, provided strong defensive support as Stokes farmed the bowling carefully and moved from watchful restraint early in his innings to ODI style aggression in this last-wicket partnership. The tension mounted as England moved closer to the target and English fans dared to hope that the seemingly impossible might be achieved. A combination of Australian mistakes and an umpiring error conspired against the visitors as England moved within the last runs of victory. First Nathan Lyon fumbled an easy run out with England still needing two. Then Australia wasted their final review on a decision which was clearly correct. This meant that they were unable to challenge umpire Joel Wilson's decision to give Stokes not out to an LBW appeal, a decision replays showed was clearly incorrect. The final runs were coming at a staggeringly fast rate compared with England's earlier painstaking progress and with just one more run needed Stokes crashed the ball to the extra cover boundary to clinch an implausible win with Leach on just 1 not out. Stokes's innings of

135 not out must rank as one of the greatest in Ashes history as he successfully delivered an England win against such odds virtually single-handedly.

England's efforts at Headingley which kept alive their chance of winning back the Ashes were soon rendered null as Smith returned at Manchester with a double hundred to give Australia a first-innings lead of 196. The Aussie pace bowlers, particularly Cummins and Hazlewood, continued at their consistently high standard and England were beaten by 185 runs. The Ashes were now out of reach, but England still had enough fight in them to improve both their batting and bowling in the final Test at the Oval and record a win by 135 runs to level the series at two games apiece. All in all, it was probably a fair result with neither side establishing sufficient overall superiority despite some tremendous individual performances. Smith's batting performance which has elevated him to second in the adjusted averages behind only Bradman is discussed further below.

5TH ERA BATSMEN

	⚑	M	R	RAW AV	ADJ AV	RAW RK	ADJ RK
S SMITH	AUS	27	2800	65.12	57.52	3	2
COOK	ENG	35	2493	40.21	33.51	33	48
PONTING	AUS	35	2476	44.21	38.01	25	32
CLARKE	AUS	35	2241	40.75	35.88	31	41
PIETERSEN	ENG	27	2158	44.95	38.96	23	28
BELL	ENG	33	1983	35.41	32.85	43	52
ROOT	ENG	24	1694	40.33	39.65	32	25
LANGER	AUS	21	1658	50.24	44.46	12	17
D WARNER	AUS	23	1615	39.39	37.10	35	37

The adjusted averages show that Smith is now ranked second only to Bradman. His performances in the two most recent series were remarkable. On only four occasions have more runs been scored by an individual in an Ashes series in Australia than the 687 scored by

Smith in 2017/18 (three times by Englishmen, Hammond, Cook and Sutcliffe and once by Bradman) and Smith's raw average of 137.4 and adjusted average of 101.24 are higher than any of these (though Hutton with a smaller run aggregate of 533 in 1950/51 did have a higher adjusted average of 109.7). In 2019 Smith scored 774 runs at a lower raw average of 110.57 but a higher adjusted average of 104.07. Only two other players, Bradman and Mark Taylor have scored more runs in an Ashes series in England and Smith's adjusted average is higher than both of these.

Aged only 30, Smith might expect to play several more Ashes series and become the all-time highest run scorer. Hobbs, who is currently second to Bradman, amassed 3,636 runs, only 836 ahead of Smith's current tally. Bradman scored 1,392 more than Hobbs, and there seems no obvious reason why Smith might not overhaul that as well. Bradman himself was within a week of his 30th birthday when the last Ashes Test before the second World War was played and it was more than eight years before the next Ashes Test in late 1946 which meant he had the chance to play only a further ten matches before his last match in 1948. This underlines the magnitude of Bradman's achievements and if Smith were to score enough Ashes runs to match Bradman it's likely he would have to score the remainder at a raw average around 130 to challenge Bradman's overall adjusted average. Even his dedication can surely not deliver this though if he can continue in anything like his present vein he can expect to cement his position of number 2 in the adjusted rankings.

Of the other batsmen still playing, Root has now entered the list of core players with an adjusted ranking of 25, as has Warner with a ranking of 37 that has been adversely affected by a disastrous 2019 series in which he scored less than 100 runs from ten completed innings.

Of the 11 series played this century, seven show much higher runs per wicket than the historic average of 28.9 and most players find their figures adjusted downwards as a result. Cook is particularly affected because such a high percentage of his runs came in high scoring games at Brisbane, Adelaide and Sydney in 2010/11 and Melbourne in 2017/18.

5TH ERA BOWLERS

Apart from Glenn McGrath and Shane Warne, whose careers were split between Eras 4 and 5, the bowlers in this era meeting the qualification threshold so far are Jimmy Anderson, Stuart Broad, Mitchell Johnson, Nathan Lyon and Peter Siddle. Some other players from this era are mentioned in Chapter 6, where we look at current players, and some of these are also mentioned briefly in Chapter 7, where we look at players who just missed the cut.

The figures for Anderson, Broad, Johnson, Lyon and Siddle are:

	⚑	M	W	RAW AV	ADJ AV	RAW RK	ADJ RK
S BROAD	ENG	32	118	29.36	27.16	33	30
ANDERSON	ENG	32	104	34.57	30.55	42	40
M JOHNSON	AUS	19	87	25.82	23.89	25	9
LYON	AUS	23	85	30.53	29.60	36	39
SIDDLE	AUS	24	80	29.81	26.84	34	27

Although Jimmy Anderson has led England's pace attack for many years, with success in the more recent Ashes series and some match winning performances, he has taken his wickets at a comparatively high cost both on a raw average and an adjusted average basis. Stuart Broad's figures are better, but he ranks behind John Snow and Fred Trueman, who are recognised as two of the all-time great English fast bowlers. Mitchell Johnson's adjusted average puts him behind only Dennis Lillee and Craig McDermott among the genuinely fast bowlers through the ages. The other pace bowlers above him, Glenn McGrath, Terry Alderman and Maurice Tate were fast-medium bowlers, who relied more on seam movement or swing.

4TH/5TH ERA SPLIT

One batsman, Nasser Hussain, and two bowlers, Glenn McGrath and Shane Warne, had careers which straddled Eras 4 and 5 sufficiently to warrant treatment in a separate category.

Hussain's figures are:

		M	R	RAW AV	ADJ AV	RAW RK	ADJ RK
HUSSAIN	ENG	23	1581	38.56	35.12	37	42

Though his ranking is comparatively low, he is ahead of all the England batsmen in Era 4 apart from David Gower and is one of only 10 Englishmen in history to have scored a double century in an Ashes test.

The figures for Warne and McGrath are:

		M	W	RAW AV	ADJ AV	RAW RK	ADJ RK
WARNE	AUS	36	195	23.25	21.15	15	3
MCGRATH	AUS	30	157	20.92	20.39	8	2

Their contribution to Australian dominance in the 1990s and early 2000s was immense and this is reflected in their positions of second and third in the overall rankings as well as their overall tallies of wickets. Warne single-handedly revitalised leg spin bowling at Test match level, inspiring a generation of young players across the world to take it up. Consistently accurate, particularly so for a leg spinner, he could drop the ball exactly where he wanted it and yet generate so much turn that high-class Test batsmen would stare in disbelief. His influence on the game and young cricketers both in Australia and internationally was enhanced by his charisma on the field, where he won so many matches for Australia, and also by his film-star lifestyle off it. He also gained the reputation of an anti-hero thanks to transgressions against the rules and several disputes with the authorities.

As a consequence, he never captained Australia, a source of great disappointment to him.

Although he doesn't figure in Bradman's all-time Australian Ashes XI, no player from the 1990s achieves that honour. Roland Perry, author of the book explains that Bradman preferred the leg spinning duo of Clarrie Grimmett and Bill O'Reilly and quotes statistics based on raw averages and Tests against all countries up to the cut-off date for publication of August 2002. However, using figures for Ashes Tests and adjusted averages rather than raw averages, Warne wins not only on the averages but also on wickets taken per Test. This comparison between Warne, Grimmett and O'Reilly is considered in more detail in Chapter 14. Boycott includes both Warne and O'Reilly in his all-time Australian squad and includes Grimmett in the reserves. CMJ ranks Warne fourth overall, making him CMJ's greatest cricketer from either England or Australia since Bradman.

Glenn McGrath is rated 12th overall by CMJ with only Warne and Tendulkar of those playing in 2009 above him. Boycott includes McGrath along with Ray Lindwall, Dennis Lillee and Alan Davidson as the fast bowlers in his Australian squad. McGrath was not genuinely quick in the same manner as Lindwall and Lillee, but his accuracy of line and length brought him success. Boycott noted McGrath's ability to land the ball consistently on a length on middle and off to just outside off, his useful bouncer and yorker and his reliance on seam movement rather than swing. At 80% he has the highest success rate in matches played for Australia of all players featured in this book and is equalled only by George Lohmann of England. The significance of Warne and McGrath is perhaps underlined still further by the 89% Ashes success rate for Australia in matches in which both played.

THE CURRENT PLAYERS

Inevitably there is interest in knowing how the current players rank against the main featured players in the book and in particular the all-time greats. I've decided to interpret "current" to include anyone who played in the 2010/11 and/or subsequent series and to drop the qualification threshold for batsmen to 500 runs with at least 14 completed innings. 22 batsmen meet these criteria, 11 Englishmen and eleven Australians, two of whom, Stuart Broad and Mitchell Johnson, are bowlers who also scored more than 500 runs. For bowlers to qualify they need to have taken 25 wickets and bowled at least 200 overs. Fourteen players meet those criteria, six Englishmen and eight Australians.

The players are listed in the tables below in order of adjusted average. The ADJ RK column applies only to players who meet the overall qualifying conditions and the figure shown is their overall ranking among the core players. The ADJ RK N column applies to all other players and shows where that individual would rank among the core players if he (but not the other current non-core players) were included.

TABLE OVERLEAF

CURRENT BATSMEN

	🏳	ADJ AV	ADJ RK	ADJ RK N	M	R	RAW AV
S SMITH	AUS	57.52	2		27	2800	65.12
ROGERS	AUS	48.63		13	15	1310	48.52
HUSSEY	AUS	48.53		13	15	1304	59.27
TROTT	ENG	42.80		22	12	917	48.26
STOKES	ENG	40.47		23	14	921	38.38
ROOT	ENG	39.65	25		24	1694	40.33
WATSON	AUS	39.03		28	19	1487	42.49
PIETERSEN	ENG	38.96	28		27	2158	44.95
PONTING	AUS	38.01	32		35	2476	44.21
D WARNER	AUS	37.10	37		23	1615	39.39
HADDIN	AUS	36.97		38	20	1366	41.39
CLARKE	AUS	35.88	41		35	2241	40.75
STRAUSS	ENG	35.39		42	20	1421	39.47
COOK	ENG	33.51	48		35	2493	40.21
BELL	ENG	32.85	52		33	1983	35.41
KATICH	AUS	27.36		62	13	701	31.86
BAIRSTOW	ENG	27.08		62	19	890	26.97
KHAWAJA	AUS	25.94		62	12	627	29.86
PRIOR	ENG	24.90		62	18	753	28.96
COLLINGWOOD	ENG	22.82		62	16	783	30.11
M JOHNSON	AUS	20.20		62	19	533	19.74
S BROAD	ENG	19.24		62	32	899	19.98

CURRENT BOWLERS

		ADJ AV	ADJ RK	ADJ RK N	M	W	RAW AV
CUMMINS	AUS	20.34		2	10	52	21.85
HARRIS	AUS	20.64		3	12	57	20.63
M JOHNSON	AUS	23.89	9		19	87	25.82
HAZLEWOOD	AUS	24.20		13	13	57	24.44
BRESNAN	ENG	24.79		15	7	26	27.58
STARC	AUS	26.34		23	13	55	28.18
SIDDLE	AUS	26.84	27		24	80	29.81
S BROAD	ENG	27.16	30		32	118	29.36
HILFENHAUS	AUS	28.97		39	9	29	35.13
LYON	AUS	29.60	39		23	85	30.53
ANDERSON	ENG	30.55	40		32	104	34.57
FINN	ENG	30.91		41	7	28	30.39
SWANN	ENG	34.61		44	18	62	39.98
STOKES	ENG	37.21		44	14	34	35.94

There are a few general points emerging from this:
- Australia are far superior in both batting and bowling.
- Among the batsmen, Steve Smith is second in the core rankings and Chris Rogers and Mike Hussey, outside the core players, each have a notional ranking of 13, well above England's leading player, Trott at 22.
- Among the bowlers not only does Mitchell Johnson have a core adjusted ranking of 9, Pat Cummins and Ryan Harris, outside the core players, have adjusted averages of 20.34 and 20.64 respectively, giving them notional rankings of second and third overall. If Cummins could maintain his current strike rate of wickets per match and his current adjusted average in the next Ashes series he would enter the core rankings as the top Australian bowler with an average just 0.05 better than McGrath. England's leading player Bresnan has a notional ranking of 15.

On the subject of current Australian superiority it should be noted that despite winning more of the last nine series than Australia, England were whitewashed 5-0 in both 2006/07 and 2013/14 (this has only happened on one other occasion in Ashes history, in 1920/21 when England had not recovered from the effects of the First World War) and lost the 2017/18 series 4-0.

The old adage is that it is bowlers who win matches. Since 2000 Australia at different times have had Glenn McGrath, Shane Warne, Mitchell Johnson, Ryan Harris, Mitchell Starc, Josh Hazlewood and Pat Cummins. England have rarely had bowlers with equivalent impact nor batsmen of the stature to resist the Australian onslaught. There are also the matters of resilience and the "killer instinct". In recent years, Australia have often seemed stronger on both counts. These characteristics manifested themselves in the Baggy Greens being harder to beat when it seemed England should have had the upper hand, and Australia driving home their advantage more strongly when *they* had the upper hand. Headingley in 2019 was an exception to that but this was largely due to the efforts of one man, Ben Stokes, and England need to instil more of this spirit into the team ethos to maintain a more consistent challenge to the Aussies.

Rarely in recent series have England been able to match Australian bowling for pure pace and although this has been less significant in English conditions where the fast medium pace of Anderson and Broad allied to movement through the air and off the seam have been effective, in Australia it is extra pace which has been conclusive. Jofra Archer is now an exciting addition to England's armoury and English fans must hope that his talent will bear fruit in Australia in 2021/22. In recent series the lack of a top-class spin bowler has also been significant. Moeen Ali, England's recent first choice spinner until Lord's in 2019, has been disappointing with only 20 wickets from 11 matches at a high average whereas Nathan Lyon is a fully effective front-line off spinner with 85 wickets from 23 matches at an adjusted average far better for example than that of Graeme Swann England's last effective front line spinner.

Among the batsmen, Smith has now become something of an icon and his recent match-winning performances have been discussed in Chapter 6. Although he may never surpass Bradman's overall career average his last two series taken together show a better raw average and adjusted average than Bradman achieved in any two consecutive series. Currently Smith is a barrier to English success comparable with the barrier Bradman represented in the 1930s. It seems that the damage to his reputation from the ball-tampering disgrace in South Africa, also discussed in Chapter 6, has been somewhat diluted by the passage of time, his grit and courage through his concussion at Lord's and his sheer dedication to cricket and to his batting. Warner, who was considered more culpable in the ball-tampering incident has perhaps seen his reputation recover more slowly but nevertheless he presented a more likeable image to fans during the 2019 series than he had previously. Behind Smith, with high notional rankings, of 13 in each case, for Australia are Chris Rogers and Mike Hussey whereas England's two leaders, Trott and Root are further behind with rankings of 22 and 25 respectively, Trott's being notional.

There are others whose adjusted averages are as good or better than some players who would be included in all-time Ashes teams. As we'll discuss in Chapter 13, players such as Hammond and Compton are commonly included in all-time Ashes XIs for very understandable reasons but have much lower individual Ashes rankings. Do any of the current batsmen other than Smith merit comparison with Hammond and Compton? Root ranks 25th in the adjusted averages and suffers from a weakness in converting 50s into hundreds. Kevin Pietersen was the batsman most widely considered to have the greatest natural talent. In the overall adjusted averages he ranks 28th, a little above Compton at 31st but well below Hammond at 20th. And Pietersen's personality often had a negative, rather than positive, impact on the England side. If anyone in the more recent series deserves praise for motivational qualities it is perhaps Michael Clarke who, notwithstanding his disappointing 2015 series, played a number of innings which delivered wins for Australia. Although his adjusted average sees him fall well below Pietersen and Compton, his seven centuries in 35 matches is better than Pietersen, who scored four centuries in 27 games, Alastair Cook, who has scored five in 35, Ian Bell, who scored four in 33 and Root with just three from 24 games. Looking back just a little further Ponting who last played in the 2010/11 series is close to Pietersen and Compton in adjusted average and has one more century than Clarke also from 35 matches.

One England batsman who narrowly fails to meet the conditions for inclusion in Chapter 8 and can't be considered 'current' as his ten-match Ashes career finished in 2005 is Michael Vaughan. With 959 runs he has a raw average of 47.95 and an adjusted average of 40.71 which would put him at 23 in the overall rankings. His record of four centuries from ten matches is better than any England batsman, although ten matches is a small number from which to draw really reliable conclusions. His biggest contributions were his inspirational batting in the 2002/03 series when he was the one English success and his performance as captain in 2005, when he revitalised England and secured the Ashes for the first time in 19 years.

Comment should be made about Alastair Cook, Jimmy Anderson and Stuart Broad, senior England players all of whom have played in six series or more against Australia. Cook, who retired from Test cricket after the series against India in 2018 (with scores of 71 and 147 in his last match) is England's leading run scorer in Test matches by a margin of more than 3,500 runs. However, he has performed less well against Australia, than in Test matches overall, with a raw average of less than 30 in four of his seven series. His raw average in all Tests is 45.35 but is just 40.21 in Ashes Tests, boosted by his series aggregate of 766 at a raw average of 127.7 in 2010/11. However, this raw average of 40.21 falls further to 33.51 when adjusted, dropping him to 48 in the adjusted rankings.

In September 2018 Anderson overtook Glenn McGrath to become the all-time highest Test wicket taker among pace bowlers and now has 575 wickets. There are just three bowlers, all spinners, who have taken more wickets. Anderson is regarded as one of England's greatest ever bowlers and so it may seem surprising that in the adjusted averages for Ashes bowlers he ranks at only 40 (the lowest of the England pace bowlers) out of the 43 bowlers meeting the full qualification conditions. Relative to his overall performance in Test matches Anderson has not fared well against Australia, with a raw bowling average in excess of 40 in three series. His overall Ashes raw average is 34.57 (26.94 for Tests against all countries) and although this is reduced to 30.55 by the adjustment mechanism, that is still a run and a half per wicket more than Bob Willis who is just above him at 38 in the rankings.

Compare that with Broad, who with 467 wickets is now second to Anderson in the table of all-time England Test wicket takers. Broad's raw average in Ashes Tests is 29.36 (28.67 for Tests against all countries) improving to 27.16 on an adjusted basis to give him a rank of 30th overall, four places behind Bedser and well ahead of Botham, Willis and Anderson.

PLAYERS WHO JUST MISSED THE CUT

Among those who failed to meet the qualification conditions of 1,500 runs for batsmen and 75 wickets for bowlers there are many fascinating players who turned in remarkable performances which won matches and seized headlines for a period of time. Some of them have already been discussed when we explored matches across the eras.

In this section, I've selected some of these players and calculated their adjusted averages on the same basis as for the players who met the qualification criteria. There is an element of subjectivity in the players selected; however to avoid undue distortion of results from just a few magnificent performances, all players shown have achieved either 1,000 runs or 50 wickets. You can see their raw and adjusted statistics in the table below and to aid comparison with the core players the final column shows what the adjusted average ranking would be for those selected if they were included with the core players.

TABLE OVERLEAF

MISSED THE CUT BATSMEN

		ERA	M	R	RAW AV	ADJ AV	ADJ RK N
HAYDEN	AUS	5	20	1461	45.65	41.78	22
KJHUGHES	AUS	4	22	1499	38.43	42.15	22
HUSSEY	AUS	5	15	1304	59.27	48.53	13
JACKSON	ENG	1	20	1415	48.79	54.34	4
DMJONES	AUS	4	17	1320	50.76	43.71	19
ROGERS	AUS	5	15	1310	48.52	48.63	13
SHREWSBURY	ENG	1	23	1277	35.47	52.73	7
SIMPSON	AUS	3	19	1405	50.17	39.16	28
STACKPOLE	AUS	3	13	1164	50.60	48.91	13
STRAUSS	ENG	5	20	1421	39.47	35.39	42
THORPE	ENG	4	16	1235	45.74	45.59	15

MISSED THE CUT BOWLERS

		ERA	M	W	RAW AV	ADJ AV	ADJ RK N
W BARNES	ENG	1	21	51	15.54	23.11	7
BATES	ENG	1	15	50	16.42	23.67	8
COTTER	AUS	1	16	67	28.60	30.15	40
CUMMINS	AUS	5	10	52	21.85	20.34	2
GOUGH	ENG	4	17	74	30.81	30.83	41
HARRIS	AUS	5	12	57	20.63	20.64	3
HAZLEWOOD	AUS	5	13	57	24.44	24.20	13
HOGG	AUS	4	11	56	17.00	22.25	5
LARWOOD	ENG	2	15	64	29.87	24.92	16
MALLETT	AUS	3	16	50	31.62	31.11	41
STARC	AUS	5	13	55	28.18	26.34	23
STATHAM	ENG	3	22	69	30.98	32.31	42
SWANN	ENG	5	18	62	39.98	34.61	44
VERITY	ENG	2	18	59	28.06	24.68	15

Among the batsmen I could not leave out Kim Hughes who fell just one run short of the qualification condition and Matthew Hayden, Michael Hussey, Dean Jones, Chris Rogers, Bobby Simpson, Keith Stackpole and Graham Thorpe all had raw averages above 45.

Andrew Strauss, England's last-but-one captain is of obvious interest and from Era 1, Jackson's raw average of over 48 looked worthy of examination. Arthur Shrewsbury's raw figures are very close to those of WG Grace.

Among the bowlers, Billy Bates and Billy Barnes from Era 1 have raw averages similar to their contemporaries Bobby Peel and Charlie Turner, and Darren Gough was just one wicket short of meeting the qualification criteria. English pace bowlers are under-represented among the core bowlers compared to those from Australia so it seemed right to include with Gough not just Harold Larwood for his reputation and notoriety gained during the Bodyline tour, but also Brian Statham who bolstered England's pace attack in the 1950s. I would have liked also to include Frank Tyson given that he was considered by many to be England's fastest ever bowler for a short period in the 1954/55 series but with only 32 wickets overall I couldn't justify this.

Hedley Verity warrants inclusion because of his high critical acclaim particularly from Don Bradman, and Rodney Hogg for his low raw average and magnificent performance in the 1978/79 series when Australia were struggling, having lost players to Packer's WSC. Ryan Harris who enjoyed outstanding success in 2013 and 2013/14 is included to emphasise his outstanding figures but is also discussed in Chapters 6 and 7. In addition to Harris I have included Mitchell Starc still a current force for Australia although he was selected for only one match in the 2019 Ashes.

'Tibby' Cotter is included as he was the fastest Australian Test bowler in the early 1900s and, but for his refusal to go on the 1912 tour for the reasons discussed in Chapter 2, would very likely have reached the qualification condition of 75 wickets.

As to the results, the two batsmen of note are Stanley Jackson and Arthur Shrewsbury, both from Era 1. Both of them have an adjusted average higher than WG Grace's 50.66, which is ninth overall for the core players and the highest of the core players from Era 1. Shrewsbury played his first test in Australia in 1881/82 and his last in England in 1893. Primarily a back-foot player, known for his straight bat and tremendous discipline and concentration, he was highly regarded by WG Grace. Shrewsbury was the first player to amass 1,000 runs in Test cricket and held the individual series aggregate record for a number of years before being overtaken by the Australians Joe Darling and Clem Hill. He captained England in seven Tests, five of which were won. Shrewsbury's adjusted average of 52.73 is slightly higher than that of WG Grace, although he had an advantage over WG in that he was just 21 years of age when the first Test against Australia was played and thus had the opportunity to play more matches against them in his prime. In 1899, RH Lyttleton praises the correctness of Shrewsbury's play, writing: "the whole of his method on a difficult wicket is a perfect study. In my humble judgment on such wickets he has never been excelled by any cricketer and has only been equalled by Grace". Shrewsbury made three centuries in his 1,277 runs including a magnificent 164 on a rain-affected pitch at Lord's in 1886, which led England to a total of 353 and victory by an innings and 106 runs.

Jackson (who later become Sir Stanley following a political career in which he was Financial Secretary to the War Office before going to India as Governor of Bengal) has figures which are even more admirable. With an adjusted average of 54.34 he would be 4th in the overall adjusted rankings. Jackson first played for England in 1883 while still at Cambridge University, making 91 on his debut. Other commitments meant that he was never able to tour Australia but he played 20 Tests in England, the last being in 1905. He captained England to a 2-0 victory in that series (winning the toss all five times) and topped both the batting averages (492 runs at 70.28) and the bowling averages (13 wickets at 15.46). Lyttleton, again writing in 1899, said of Jackson: "At the present, indeed, he stands in quite the first rank of cricketers, whether English or Colonials, and I am inclined to think that, if I had to choose a side, my first choice would be Jackson".

Moving to the bowlers, Bates played 15 Tests for England between 1881 and 1887, all of which were in Australia. A right-arm off-break bowler, his raw average was similar to those of Turner and Peel but his adjusted average was, at 23.67, significantly better and would have placed him at eighth in the overall rankings and first among the

Era 1 bowlers. His greatest bowling performance was at Melbourne in 1882/83 when he became the first bowler to take a Test match hat-trick. His match figures of 14 for 102 took England to the first ever innings victory in Test matches between the two countries. Only Wilfred Rhodes, with 15 wickets at Melbourne in 1903/04, has taken as many as 14 wickets in an England v Australia match in Australia. Billy Barnes, a right-arm fast-medium bowler also playing for England in the 1880s had an adjusted average which was slightly better still and his three five wicket hauls were all in the Australian second innings securing England victories. Both Barnes and Bates were also strong batsmen and are discussed in Chapter 9 on all-rounders.

The other England bowler in this list with a high adjusted ranking is left-arm slow bowler Hedley Verity, who bowled left-arm spin at a faster-than-normal pace and with great accuracy. He was able to maintain this accuracy even in the face of fierce punishment from batsmen which occasionally happened to him on the very best batting tracks. Verity's greatest performance was his 15 for 104 at Lords in 1934, during which he dismissed Bradman twice and guided England to an innings victory and their first win at Lord's over Australia since 1896. (England would not beat Australia again at the home of cricket until 2009.) In total he dismissed Bradman eight times in Tests, more than any other English bowler and Bradman never felt that he mastered him. Based on his own experience of Verity, Bradman selected him ahead of Jim Laker for the one spin bowling place in his all-time England Ashes XI. Verity played just 18 matches between the wars before dying during World War Two after being wounded during the invasion of Sicily. Batsman dominated that second era and the adjustment mechanism reduces Verity's average to 24.68, which would have placed him at 15th in the adjusted list. Other than Verity (and Laker, Underwood and Emburey who are included in the core bowlers) there is only one other England slow bowler since era 1 who has taken over 50 wickets and this is Graham Swann. Although his adjusted average would give him a ranking below any of the core players he nevertheless was a key part of the England attack and was a match winner for England on several occasions.

Of the trio of England pace bowlers who just missed out, Gough and Statham have fairly high adjusted averages, which would place them well towards the bottom of the core bowler listing had they achieved the qualifying conditions. Though successful wicket takers, their raw averages show this was achieved at some cost and the small adjustment indicates that the matches they played in had average runs per wicket close to the overall amount.

Larwood played in the era of batting dominance and the adjustment brings his average down to the area where many of the bowlers are clustered, better than Trueman and close to Snow. Of course with Larwood it is very much a career of two different phases, the first before Bodyline when he was not particularly effective and the Bodyline tour itself where he was devastating. He was not selected again, effectively being made the scapegoat for the perceived wrongs of the tactics, widely considered to be an unjust action by the English cricket authorities who knew that Larwood was following the instructions given to him by his team captain, Douglas Jardine.

Rodney Hogg took 41 wickets at a raw average of 12.85 in the 1978/79 series, still a record series aggregate for an Australian against England in Australia. Hogg was far and away the most successful bowler for the hosts in this series, which England won 5-1 against an Australian side which really amounted to a second XI such was the loss of players to Packer's WSC. Hogg's remaining 15 wickets against England were spread over two series in 1981 and 1982/83 and his adjusted average of 22.25 places him behind Alderman but ahead of Lillee.

The more recent Australian pace bowlers featured here also compare well with the best across the ages. Pat Cummins with a notional position of second overall would lead all the Australian bowlers and Ryan Harris, with a notional position of third overall, would be ahead of all save Glenn McGrath (the number one overall position being filled by Jim Laker, an off-spinner). Starc, although being behind many earlier Australian pace bowlers, and half a run behind Peter Siddle who is now among the core bowlers, compares favourably with many of England's pace bowlers.

Ashley Mallet from era 3 also shown in the table, with 50 wickets and a notional ranking of 41, is the only other Australian off spinner since WW2 to have taken as many as 50 wickets.

THE ALL-ROUNDERS

Just four players, Monty Noble, Wilfred Rhodes, Keith Miller and Ian Botham achieved the qualification conditions for both batsmen and bowlers. To those four I have added Warwick Armstrong and George Giffen, both of whom achieved 1,000 runs and 50 wickets. The figures for these six (whom I consider to be the core all-rounders, that is the equivalent of the 61 batsmen and 43 bowlers discussed in earlier chapters) are as follows:

ALL-ROUNDERS BATTING

		ERA	M	R	RAW AV	ADJ AV	RAW RK	ADJ RK
ARMSTRONG	AUS	1	42	2172	35.03	37.11	45	36
NOBLE	AUS	1	39	1905	30.72	33.52	56	47
RHODES	ENG	1	41	1706	31.01	33.51	54	49
BOTHAM	ENG	4	36	1673	29.35	32.00	59	55
MILLER	AUS	3	29	1511	33.57	33.67	48	46
GIFFEN	AUS	1	31	1238	23.35	26.14	N/A	N/A

TABLE OVERLEAF

ALL-ROUNDERS BOWLING

	⚑	ERA	M	W	RAW AV	ADJ AV	RAW RK	ADJ RK
BOTHAM	ENG	4	36	148	27.65	28.37	31	34
NOBLE	AUS	1	39	115	24.86	28.33	20	33
RHODES	ENG	1	41	109	24.00	27.88	17	32
GIFFEN	AUS	1	31	103	27.09	33.24	29	43
MILLER	AUS	3	29	87	22.40	24.20	13	12
ARMSTRONG	AUS	1	42	74	30.91	31.79	N/A	N/A

Armstrong is first of the all-rounders in the adjusted averages for batting and Miller for bowling. The latter's bowling ranking of 12th puts him ahead of all the core England pace bowlers other than Tate and his adjusted average of 24.20 is more than 3.5 runs per wickets ahead of Noble, Rhodes and Botham who are all within half a run of each other. Armstrong leads the batting from Miller, Noble and Rhodes with Botham not far behind. Of the six, Giffen was the first to play Test cricket making his debut in 1881 and playing his last game in 1896, two years before Noble made his debut.

Giffen, who was an attacking right-handed batsman and an accurate slow-medium off-break bowler, was widely considered to be one of the greatest Australian cricketers to play before Bradman and he frequently dominated the State games in which he played. His Test career was less successful and fell into two distinct phases; the period up to 1886 and the period from 1891. In his 17 Tests up to 1886, by which time he was 27 years old, he had scored just 463 runs at an adjusted average of 22 and had taken 29 wickets at an adjusted average of 44. Hardly sparkling figures for a cricketer of such repute. He played no Test cricket again until 1891 due to disagreements with the authorities over both payment and the selection of his brother Walter.

He returned for Australia in 1891/92 and then played in 14 consecutive Tests until his last on the tour of England in 1896 when he was 37. In these 14 tests he made 775 runs at an adjusted average of 30.47 and took 74 wickets at an adjusted average of 29.03, figures which compare more favourably with the results of the other five all-rounders and better reflect his acknowledged abilities. In the process he became the first cricketer to do the double of 1,000 runs and 100 wickets in Tests.

Noble, who made his Test debut on New Year's Day 1898, ranks highly among Ashes wicket takers. Only six players have taken more wickets than his 115 in Ashes tests and only two Australians have taken more wickets in a match than his 13-77 at Melbourne in 1901/02. He also had eight-wicket and seven-wicket match hauls in that series which helped Australia to a 4-1 series win. All told he took ten wickets in a match twice and five wickets in an innings nine times. He bowled at medium pace and was penetrating enough to open the bowling in about a third of the Tests in which he played. As a batsman he made just one century but reached 50 a further 15 times and opened the batting for Australia in the 1907/08 series in which he was also captain, leading his side to a 4-1 series win. In all he captained Australia in three series, in two of which they emerged as series winners.

Born seven months after the first Test match was played in 1877, Wilfred Rhodes made his Ashes debut at Trent Bridge in 1899 in the last match in which WG Grace played. By the time he finished his Test career aged 52, he had broken WG's record as the oldest English Test cricketer, although WG still holds the record for Ashes Tests. With a tally of 4,187, Rhodes remains the all-time leading wicket taker in first class cricket, and only 17 batsmen have scored more than his run tally of 39,802.

He made his mark for Yorkshire and England initially as a slow left-arm bowler having spent months of solitary practice to master length and flight. After his debut in the 1899 Ashes series he was unable to tour Australia in 1901/02 because he was directed by Lord Hawke the Captain and President of Yorkshire to refuse the invitation. At Edgbaston in 1902 Rhodes took 7-17 to reduce Australia to an innings total of 36 which remains their lowest ever score in Test matches. At Melbourne in 1903/04 he took 15-124 to help England win by 185 runs. Jim Laker with his 19-90 in 1956 at Manchester is the only Englishman to have taken more wickets in a Test and no-one else, either English or Australian, has taken as many as 15 wickets in an Ashes test in Australia.

Rhodes took 31 wickets in that series helping England to a 3-2 series win. At the time he was batting low down the order but his ability was starting to flourish. In the first Test in 1903/04, batting at number 11 he scored 40 not out, adding 130 in a record last-wicket stand with 'Tip' Foster. Rhodes was a cautious batsman with a sound defence. A typical Yorkshireman he was hard to get out, and by the 1911-12 series he was opening the batting with Jack Hobbs. In the fourth Test at Melbourne they put on 323 for the first wicket, with Rhodes making 179, his only century against Australia. Both the 130 last-wicket stand and the 323 first-wicket stand remain as records for England against Australia. In all Rhodes opened the batting with Hobbs in 11 of the 41 tests he played against Australia. Rhodes was recalled to play his last Test against Australia in 1926 at the age of 48 and he took 4-44 in the second innings to secure victory for England and the return of the Ashes for the first time since 1912.

Armstrong was a capable, though not attractive, batsman and an outstandingly accurate leg-break bowler. At 6ft 3ins tall he was of slim build when he made his Test debut in the 1901/02 series. However, in his last two Test match series after the war, in 1920/21 and 1921, for both of which he was captain, his weight had increased to over 20 stone, earning him the nickname The Big Ship. He delivered many key performances in the Australian series-winning sides of 1907/08 and 1909 and his success percentage of 90 in his ten games as captain following World War One has not been bettered by any Australian captain other than three players who skippered the country for two Tests or fewer. Steve Smith, Australia's captain in the Ashes series in 2017/18, also has a success percentage of 90, although this is based on only a single home series.

Whilst Noble, Rhodes and Armstrong were contemporaries at the time Ashes cricket was developing, Miller played in a much-changed era. By the time he came on the scene in 1946/47 there had been two world wars, the dominance of batsmen in the inter-war years and a number of rule changes. Between Miller's last Ashes test in 1956 and Botham's Ashes debut, 20 years elapsed and times changed again. Nevertheless, the pair had a lot in common. Both were fast bowlers, aggressive batsmen and larger-than-life characters who were capable of performances that changed the course of Ashes Tests, whose names have come up automatically in our earlier discussions about the history of the Ashes.

They were both players whose contributions were far greater than can be determined from any set of averages, raw or adjusted. One also has to look at their match-winning performances. For Miller some of this has been covered in Chapter 4 where his bowling as part of Australia's opening partnership with Ray Lindwall is discussed together with his war-time experiences and his general approach to the game. His debut came in the first post-War Ashes Test at Brisbane in 1946/47. He made 79 and took nine wickets to give Australia victory by an innings and 332 runs as England were caught twice on a rain affected pitch. Showing his versatility, as the conditions changed from a green wicket providing lift for the seam bowlers, to a Brisbane sticky, Miller reduced his pace and bowled off cutters taking seven wickets in the first innings and two in the second. The first of his three centuries against England came in the fourth Test of this series when his 141 not out gave Australia a small first innings lead and prevented England gaining the upper hand. His highest was 145 not out at Sydney in the third Test in 1950/51, which helped Australia to victory by an innings and 13 runs, their third consecutive win, clinching the Ashes again.

Botham made his debut in 1977 playing in two games of that series which England won 3-0. He secured five wickets in the first innings of each match he played, helping England to victory by seven wickets and by an innings and 85 runs. He then took 23 wickets and made two half-centuries in the 1978/79 series, which England won 5-1 against an Australia devoid of their WSC players. In the three-match non-Ashes series in Australia in 1979/80, which England lost 3-0 to Australia with their WSC players restored, Botham continued his strong performances with an 11-wicket match haul and his first century.

It was the 1981 series in England which contained his greatest performances. As mentioned in Chapter 5, he was captain for the first two matches, of which England drew one and lost one, and he performed badly with bat and ball collecting a "pair" at Lord's in the second Test. Realising that England would be better served by another captain, he resigned and was replaced by Mike Brearley, who had captained England in the three previous Ashes series. Botham subsequently delivered match-winning performances for England in the next three Tests and and took ten wickets in the final match, which was drawn.

The first of these performances was in the dramatic Headingley Test, which England won by just 18 runs after following on (only the second time in Ashes history this has happened). Despite 6-95 from Botham in Australia's first innings the tourists amassed 401. Botham then top scored with 50 in England's reply but they were dismissed for a mere 174, a full 227 runs behind. England, did not fare well for much of their second innings and when Botham came to the crease the score was 105-5. Before long it was 135-7. However, Graham Dilley, with 56, and Chris Old, with 29, gave Botham strong support as he savaged the bowling to reach his century off 87 balls, eventually finishing on 149 not out as England closed at 356 setting Australia 130 to win.

Few really thought Australia would fail to achieve such a modest target, particularly when they reached 56-1. However, Brearley switched Bob Willis to the Kirkstall Lane end to bowl downwind and Australia collapsed to 74-8. A brief revival saw them reach 110-8 before Willis had Dennis Lillee caught by Mike Gatting and then yorked Ray Bright to finish with 8-43 with Australia 18 short of their target. Botham finished with 199 runs for once out, seven wickets for 109 and two catches (one off his own bowling).

In the fourth Test he took five for 11 in the second innings to help dismiss Australia for 121, securing victory by the narrow margin of 29 runs. In the fifth Test with England having batted first, Botham came in at number seven in the second innings with the score at 104-5 and a lead of just 205. His century guided England to a total of 404 which helped secure a win by 103 runs in a match in which he also took five wickets. Seldom in Ashes history has an all-rounder so dominated a series.

Botham took 31 wickets in the 1985 series which England won 2-1 and played in four matches in the 1986/87 series (injury forced him to miss the match at Adelaide) making key contributions (138 at Brisbane and 5-41 in the first innings at Melbourne) in the two England victories.

His all-round cricket also extended to magnificent close-to-the-wicket fielding, his particularly quick reactions enabling him to stand closer than most to the wicket in the slip cordon, and he took significantly more catches, 57 in 36 matches, than any other England non-wicket keeper in Tests against Australia. The nearest to him was Wally Hammond, often considered England's premier slip fielder, who took 43 catches in 33 matches. At 56.9%, the success rate in the matches in which Botham played is only exceeded by six other players of whom only two, Sutcliffe and Emburey played after era 1.

CMJ rates Rhodes no 15, Miller no 16 and Botham no 18 in his top 100 but has no place for Noble. Boycott includes both Rhodes and Botham in his England squad of 14 and Miller in his Australian squad, while Bradman includes Miller in his Australian side and Botham as 12th man in his England team. He leaves out Rhodes preferring Verity, against whom he played. Neither Boycott nor Bradman have a place for Noble.

There was a dearth of all-rounders in the inter-war years and this has also been the case since Botham played his last game in 1989. However, in the same way that we looked at some batsmen and bowlers who failed to make the qualifying threshold in the previous chapter, we should also look at interesting all-rounders who have fallen a little short of the qualifying threshold. In the first edition I considered just one all-rounder, Andrew Flintoff (usually known as Freddie) in this category. He always gave an element of excitement in every game he played and scored 856 runs and took 43 wickets in his short Ashes career of 14 matches between 2005 and 2009.

Flintoff's outstanding series was in 2005 when he scored 402 runs and took 24 wickets. England won that series 2-1 but both their victories were by small margins, three wickets at Trent Bridge and just two runs at Edgbaston. In both these games Flintoff delivered the outstanding performance and this was recognised in his receipt of the Man of the Match award on both occasions. At Trent Bridge he made 102 and 26 and had match figures of 3-137 and at Edgbaston he made 68 and 73 and had match figures of 7-131. He also shared the Man of the Series award with Shane Warne.

In the recent 2019 series an all-rounder Ben Stokes was one of the star performers and there is inevitably great interest in comparing his performance with the top all-rounders through the ages. Although he is just 28 years of age and missed the 2017/18 Ashes series through suspension he has already played the same number of games as Flintoff and has scored 921 runs and taken 34 wickets to date. However, if Flintoff and Stokes are to be included then so should others with particular claims even though they do not meet the core criteria. As with the previous chapter there is an element of subjectivity in my choices but I have looked at those players who have achieved 600 runs and 30 wickets and made a selection based on such parameters as averages, match winning/saving performances and strike rate of wickets per match. This results in a further six players, four from England and two from Australia, only one of whom, Tony Greig, played after the Second World War. The figures for these additional eight players are:

ADDITIONAL ALL-ROUNDERS BATTING

	⚑	ERA	MATCHES	RUNS	RAW AV	ADJ AV	RAW RK N	ADJ RK N
STOKES	ENG	5	14	921	38.38	40.47	38	23
FLINTOFF	ENG	5	14	856	34.24	30.80	47	58
GREIG	ENG	3	21	1303	36.19	37.81	41	33
J GREGORY	AUS	2	21	941	34.85	30.68	46	58
KELLEWAY	AUS	1/2	18	874	31.21	29.05	54	59
W BARNES	ENG	1	21	725	23.39	34.94	62	44
BATES	ENG	1	15	656	27.33	38.10	60	32
ULYETT	ENG	1	23	901	25.03	33.32	62	50

ADDITIONAL ALL-ROUNDERS BOWLING

	🏳	ERA	WKTS	RUNS	RAW AV	ADJ AV	RAW RK N	ADJ RK N
STOKES	ENG	5	14	34	35.94	37.21	44	44
FLINTOFF	ENG	5	14	43	36.12	31.84	44	41
GREIG	ENG	3	21	44	37.80	38.10	44	44
J GREGORY	AUS	2	21	70	33.77	29.41	41	39
KELLEWAY	AUS	1/2	18	37	31.22	27.91	38	33
W BARNES	ENG	1	21	51	15.55	23.11	2	7
BATES	ENG	1	15	50	16.42	23.67	2	8
ULYETT	ENG	1	23	48	20.67	29.23	7	39

Billy Barnes, Billy Bates and George Ulyett played all their cricket before 1900 with Ulyett playing in the first Test of all in March 1877.

Barnes was a cavalier batsman and medium paced bowler whose three five-wicket hauls all came in the second innings and delivered wins for England. Bates was an equally capable batsman and off break bowler who took 14 wickets at Melbourne in 1882/3, one of only five times this has been done in Ashes Tests, including the first Test match hat-trick, which led to the first ever victory by an innings in Test cricket. Tragically his career ended early when he was struck by a ball in the nets and suffered permanent eye damage. Ulyett, a confident, aggressive hard-hitting batsman and fast bowler was probably the closest England had at the time to the latter-day fast-bowling, extroverted all-rounders.

Jack Gregory, best known for his opening bowling performances together with Ted McDonald in the first two series after the First World War was no mean batsman as the figures show and Charles Kelleway, who first played before the First World War, took over as Gregory's opening bowling partner for the series in 1924/5 following McDonald's retirement.

South African born, Tony Greig, was 6 feet 7 inches tall and was fearless and resolute both in his batting and in his approach as captain in the five games he led England against Australia. He was

England's leading run scorer and joint top wicket-taker (albeit at a fairly high cost per wicket) in the tough series in Australia in 1974-5 when the pace of Lillee and Thomson delivered a 4-1 series win for the Aussies. Greig was also a superb slip fielder and the only one of the all-rounders here to have taken more catches per match than Botham. His adherence to his own sometimes unconventional view and his resolute and sometimes incautious nature meant that controversy was never far away and because of his assistance to Kerry Packer in the formulation of World Series cricket he lost first the England captaincy for the 1977 series and then his place in the side bringing his Test career to an early end at the age of 31.

Ben Stokes has become one of England's leading players and certainly the most talked about after his exploits in the 2019 series. Having been one of the key players in England's World Cup ODI win in July 2019 he moved on to the Ashes series in August, discussed in Chapter 6, and by virtue of two not-out centuries, was man of the match in two of the five games. The first of these gave England a chance of victory in the drawn game at Lord's and the second secured an amazing win by one wicket at Headingley after an unbroken last wicket stand of 76 in which his partner Jack Leach made just 1 not out. England's winning fourth innings score of 362-9 is their largest fourth innings score to win in any Test match beating their previous record of 332-7, also in an Ashes Test, at Melbourne in 1928/29.

It is hard to find a single appropriate quantitative measure to compare these 14 all-rounders but set out below are two approaches which are by no means the only ones which could be devised. First, using only the adjusted batting and bowling averages, here is a table which shows for each of them the amount by which their batting average exceeds their bowling average.

Bates and Barnes lead the way here with Miller a creditable third. The others, led by Rhodes, are some way behind with three of the players showing negative figures, Greig, Flintoff and Giffen.

BATTING AVG VS BOWLING AVG

	🏳	ERA	BATTING ADJ AV	BOWLING ADJ AV	DIFFERENCE	BATTING RANK	BOWLING RANK
BATES	ENG	1	38.10	23.67	14.43	2	2
W BARNES	ENG	1	34.94	23.11	11.82	5	1
MILLER	AUS	3	33.67	24.20	9.47	6	3
RHODES	ENG	1	33.51	27.88	5.63	8	4
ARMSTRONG	AUS	1	37.11	31.79	5.31	4	10
NOBLE	AUS	1	33.52	28.33	5.19	7	6
ULYETT	ENG	1	33.32	29.23	4.09	9	8
BOTHAM	ENG	4	32.00	28.37	3.62	10	7
STOKES	ENG	5	40.47	37.21	3.25	1	13
J GREGORY	AUS	2	30.68	29.41	1.27	12	9
KELLEWAY	AUS	1/2	29.05	27.91	1.14	13	5
GREIG	ENG	3	37.81	38.10	-0.29	3	14
FLINTOFF	ENG	5	30.80	31.84	-1.05	11	11
GIFFEN	AUS	1	26.14	33.24	-7.10	14	12

Secondly, recognising that match winning/saving performances are more valuable than strong averages, here is a table showing the number of centuries and half centuries each player scored and the number of times they took ten wickets in a match or five wickets in an innings.

TABLE OVERLEAF

MATCH WINNING & MATCH SAVING

	⚑	ERA	MATCHES	100S	50S	10W	5W	CATCHES
ARMSTRONG	AUS	1	42	4	6	0	3	37
RHODES	ENG	1	41	1	9	1	6	36
NOBLE	AUS	1	39	1	15	2	9	26
BOTHAM	ENG	4	36	4	6	2	9	57
GIFFEN	AUS	1	31	1	6	1	7	24
MILLER	AUS	3	29	3	6	1	3	20
ULYETT	ENG	1	23	1	7	0	1	16
GREIG	ENG	3	21	1	10	0	0	37
J GREGORY	AUS	2	21	1	6	0	3	30
W BARNES	ENG	1	21	1	5	0	3	19
KELLEWAY	AUS	1/2	18	1	4	0	0	12
BATES	ENG	1	15	0	5	1	4	9
FLINTOFF	ENG	5	14	1	6	0	2	4
STOKES	ENG	5	14	3	4	0	2	11

Bear in mind that in contrast to the previous table, this one is not in any order of merit. The players are simply set out in descending order of matches played. However dividing the centuries, 50s, ten-wicket and five-wicket hauls for each player by the number of matches played (I've not set out these calculations as the table would get too detailed) indicates that of the 14 all-rounders, Botham has the highest ratio per match for ten-wicket hauls and Bates for five-wicket hauls (with Botham second). Stokes is ahead for centuries (with Botham second) and Greig is ahead for 50s. Among the core all-rounders Noble is the highest for 50s (behind only Greig and Flintoff).

In looking to identify the leading all-rounder in Ashes history I must look only at the core all-rounders as only they achieved the required threshold of runs and wickets. This excludes Barnes and Bates notwithstanding their impressive figures in the two tables. Bates could perhaps have been a contender had his career not been tragically cut short.

However even if I were to include the non-core players it is still doubtful that any could have greater overall claim to top all-rounder status than Botham. Although others may have better adjusted average figures it is centuries and large wicket hauls that win matches and the table immediately above shows Botham's strengths. Taking this together with his number of match-winning performances, his overall success percentage and his number of catches, Botham has a strong claim to be considered the top all-rounder in Ashes history.

THE WICKETKEEPERS

This book would not be complete without a section on wicket keepers. However, the comparison of wicketkeepers through Ashes history raises different issues from the comparison of batsmen and bowlers.

The most common statistics quoted for wicketkeepers are total dismissals and dismissals per match. Total dismissals has some similarity with total runs scored by a batsman and total wickets taken by a bowler. Likewise, dismissals per match is similar to the average runs scored per completed innings for batsmen and average runs conceded per wicket taken for bowlers. However, there are some important differences. The average number of dismissals per match varies throughout Ashes history for a variety of reasons such as: quality of equipment, development of swing and seam bowling and changing pitch conditions. In fact a review of the figures shows that there has been a steady increase in the proportion of catches at the wicket from 1877 to the present day. However it is not feasible to adjust for this in the same way as the adjustment of averages for batsmen and bowlers because the adjusted average system used in this book is dependent on there being a reasonable number of batsmen and bowlers in each match to set the benchmark average runs per wicket for the match. In contrast there are only two wicketkeepers, one of whom we are selecting for comparison at any point and so a benchmark dismissals per wicketkeeper for the match would not be at all meaningful.

There is another obvious factor, albeit unrelated to changing conditions through Ashes history, which is easy to identify and for which it is both necessary and easy to make adjustments. This is simply that there is more opportunity for a wicketkeeper to secure maximum dismissals per match if his side bowls the opposition out twice than if his side loses by an innings or by a significant number of wickets. We can adjust for this by aggregating the number of wickets taken by an individual's team in the matches in which he keeps wicket and then dividing his total dismissals by that aggregate. This gives a number less than one and it is convenient to multiply the figure by ten so that the result represents the average number of dismissals by a wicketkeeper for every ten wickets taken by his side. For example, if a wicket keeper recorded 120 dismissals in his Ashes Test match career and the number of wickets taken by his team during the matches in which he was keeping wicket was 400, the calculation would be: 120 divided by 400 equals 0.3. Then 0.3 multiplied by 10 equals 3. Or in other words, for each ten wickets taken by the team the keeper on average would have made three dismissals.

After some consideration I have decided to use this method, rather than dismissals per match, as the primary comparison measure between the various Ashes wicketkeepers because it is independent of the number of wickets taken per match by the team, a factor over which the wicketkeeper has limited control. I have to acknowledge however that this does not adjust for variations across the years and it is to be expected that wicketkeepers in later eras will produce better figures than those in earlier eras. The qualification chosen is 50 dismissals and this produces 15 wicketkeepers ranging from Jack Blackham who kept for Australia in the very first test in 1877 through to Brad Haddin who kept for Australia in the first match of the 2015 series. It's worth stating that Blackham and Alec Stewart each played in Tests where they did not keep wicket and these matches have been ignored when calculating their wicketkeeping performance (that is any catches as fielders have been ignored in counting total dismissals and the wickets falling have been ignored in counting the tally of total wickets which is divided into total dismissals), but have been included in evaluating their batting performance.

Here are the figures, first in order of total dismissals:

TOTAL DISMISSALS

		ERA	M	D	D/M	RK/M	D/10W	RK/10W
R MARSH	AUS	3/4	42	148	3.52	4	2.03	7
HEALY	AUS	4	33	135	4.09	2	2.25	4
KNOTT	ENG	3/4	34	105	3.09	8	1.92	9
GILCHRIST	AUS	5	20	96	4.80	1	2.55	1
OLDFIELD	AUS	2	38	90	2.37	13	1.54	12
LILLEY	ENG	1	32	84	2.63	10	1.54	11
HADDIN	AUS	5	20	80	4.00	3	2.38	2
A STEWART	ENG	4	26	78	3.00	9	2.29	3
GROUT	AUS	3	22	76	3.45	6	2.18	5
EVANS	ENG	3	31	76	2.45	12	1.55	10
PRIOR	ENG	5	18	63	3.50	5	2.14	6
BLACKHAM	AUS	1	32	59	1.84	14	1.14	14
R TAYLOR	ENG	4	17	57	3.35	7	1.93	8
KELLY	AUS	1	33	55	1.67	15	1.03	15
CARTER	AUS	1/2	21	52	2.48	11	1.48	13

Although catches and stumpings are not shown separately, it is interesting to note that Bert Oldfield has the most stumpings by far at 31 representing nearly 35% of his dismissals. He played in Era 2 when a greater proportion of wickets was taken by spin bowlers than in the later eras and many of his stumpings were from the bowling of Clarrie Grimmett and Bill O'Reilly, two of the four bowlers from Era 2 who reached the qualification threshold of 75 wickets. The next highest is Dick Lilley with 19 stumpings, which constituted approximately 23% of his total dismissals. Lilley played in Era 1 when pace bowling was less developed and it was possible for a wicket keeper to stand up to many more of the leading bowlers than in later years.

Here is the table again but now in order of dismissals per match and also showing the adjusted batting average:

DISMISSALS PER MATCH

	⚑	ERA	D/M	D/10W	RK/10W	ADJ AV	ADJ RK
GILCHRIST	AUS	5	4.80	2.55	1	42.41	1
HEALY	AUS	4	4.09	2.25	4	29.54	5
HADDIN	AUS	5	4.00	2.38	2	36.97	2
R MARSH	AUS	3/4	3.52	2.03	7	28.33	6
PRIOR	ENG	5	3.50	2.14	6	24.90	8
GROUT	AUS	3	3.45	2.18	5	13.67	15
R TAYLOR	ENG	4	3.35	1.93	8	20.33	13
KNOTT	ENG	3/4	3.09	1.92	9	32.20	3
A STEWART	ENG	4	3.00	2.29	3	29.84	4
LILLEY	ENG	1	2.63	1.54	11	23.61	10
CARTER	AUS	1/2	2.48	1.48	13	27.10	7
EVANS	ENG	3	2.45	1.55	10	20.41	12
OLDFIELD	AUS	2	2.37	1.54	12	20.21	14
BLACKHAM	AUS	1	1.84	1.14	14	24.02	9
KELLY	AUS	1	1.67	1.03	15	20.61	11

Adam Gilchrist tops the list both on dismissals per match and the adjusted measure of dismissals per ten wickets. He also tops the batting average by a comfortable margin.

The adjustment mechanism particularly favours Stewart who moves from ninth to third reflecting the fact that in Stewart's time England was on the losing end of many matches with Australia losing only 13 wickets per game in the matches he kept wicket compared with an overall Ashes average of 16 per team per match. In contrast, Marsh for example, drops three places from fourth to seventh. Although England and Australia were more evenly balanced throughout his career, nevertheless England lost an average of over 17 wickets per match.

As suggested above, the modern wicketkeepers tend to have stronger figures. The top four are all from Eras 4 and 5 and the bottom three are all from Era 1, while Lilley from Era 1 just manages to edge ahead of Oldfield (though still with the same ratio to two decimal places!) from Era 2. This demonstrates that the proportion of dismissals in which wicketkeepers are involved has increased through Ashes history.

Australians feature more strongly than Englishmen with nine of the 15 wicket keepers coming from Down Under and four of the top five being Australian. The main reason is that Australia used fewer wicket keepers than England in the early years and so their keepers on average played more matches and had more chance to achieve the necessary 50 dismissals to qualify. If you exclude the five wicketkeepers from Eras 1 and 2 the position becomes even with five Australians and five Englishmen in the remaining ten.

The five from Eras 1 and 2 are the bottom five in the final table of adjusted rankings and to find the reason why the Australians dominate the table of the remaining top ten one needs to look a little further. I suggest that the main factor is that Australian pace bowlers have generally been a stronger force than English pace bowlers from Era 3 onwards, that is from 1946. The bowlers' rankings illustrate this and since, also from Era 3 onwards, the vast majority of wicket-keeping dismissals have been taken from pace bowling this has given Australia a clear advantage.

Finally, the table in order of adjusted ranking by our preferred method of dismissals per ten wickets taken.

TABLE OVERLEAF

DISMISSALS PER TEN WICKETS TAKEN

	🏳	ERA	D/10W	D/M	RK/M	ADJ AV	ADJ RK
GILCHRIST	AUS	5	2.55	4.80	1	42.41	1
HADDIN	AUS	5	2.38	4.00	3	36.97	2
A STEWART	ENG	4	2.29	3.00	9	29.84	4
HEALY	AUS	4	2.25	4.09	2	29.54	5
GROUT	AUS	3	2.18	3.45	6	13.67	15
PRIOR	ENG	5	2.14	3.50	5	24.90	8
R MARSH	AUS	3/4	2.03	3.52	4	28.33	6
R TAYLOR	ENG	4	1.93	3.35	7	20.33	13
KNOTT	ENG	3/4	1.92	3.09	8	32.20	3
EVANS	ENG	3	1.55	2.45	12	20.41	12
LILLEY	ENG	1	1.54	2.63	10	23.61	10
OLDFIELD	AUS	2	1.54	2.37	13	20.21	14
CARTER	AUS	1/2	1.48	2.48	11	27.10	7
BLACKHAM	AUS	1	1.14	1.84	14	24.02	9
KELLY	AUS	1	1.03	1.67	15	20.61	11

THE CAPTAINS

To compare captains across Ashes history we need to make further changes to our approach.

The starting point is the choice of basic comparison between captains before deciding if some additional adjustment needs to be made for comparison across the eras. A quantitative measure of success is needed and for the reasons given below I have used the success percentage measure as defined in the introduction under which one point is awarded for a win and half a point for a draw. The aggregate points are then divided by the number of games (which of course is also the maximum number of points) and the result expressed as a percentage. It is true that this does not give any special reward for wins. However, it is relevant, especially in making comparisons across the eras, to note that there have been variations throughout Ashes history in how easy it is to secure a result and also variations at particular times between matches in England and Australia. For example, there were no drawn games in Australia between March 1882 and January 1947 because games were played to a finish sometimes taking as long as seven days. Conversely, matches in England were played over three days until 1926 and over four days from the following series in England in 1930 (although the last match of the series was played to a finish between 1926 and 1938) As a result 29 of the 64 Tests played in England over this period were drawn. After World War Two games lasted for the same duration, six five-hour days in Australia and five six-hour days in England.

Any method which disproportionately favoured wins would therefore advantage those captains who played games in Australia in Eras 1 and 2 and disadvantage those who played games in England during the same period. Allocating just one point for a win and half a point for a draw mitigates any such unfairness. On this basis I've concluded that the success percentage gives the best comparison that I can find.

However, of all the quantitative measures discussed in this book, a measure for captaincy is likely to be the least valuable if seen in isolation because in achieving results a captain depends more on the abilities of his teammates than batsmen and bowlers do. Even wicketkeepers, who clearly depend on bowlers, arguably have more ability to achieve results through their own actions. Furthermore, in recent years the process of team selection, development and structure of fitness and training as led by the off-field coaches has played an ever-increasing role in the game arguably reducing the role of the captain.

The record of the England and Australian captains is shown in tabular format at the end of the book.

ENGLAND

Between the captaincies of professionals Arthur Shrewsbury, who captained England for the last time in 1887, and Hutton, who captained England against Australia for the first time in 1953, all the England captains were amateurs. In the early years, many of these amateur captains were from the traditional upper classes and were not necessarily the strongest batsmen or bowlers but generally had strong leadership qualities. At the time the main part of the bowling was provided by the professionals and the primary skill of the amateur players tended to be batting. In all from 1877 to 2019 England have used 54 captains in Tests against Australia of which 19 have been captain in fewer than five matches.

In the first era from 1877 to 1912 17 captains were used as the following table shows:

1ST ERA ENGLAND CAPTAINS

	SPAN	MATCHES	WON	LOST	DRAWN	%
LILLYWHITE	1877	2	1	1	0	50
HARRIS	1879-84	4	2	1	1	63
SHAW	1881-82	4	0	2	2	25
HORNBY	1882-84	2	0	1	1	25
BLIGH	1882-83	4	2	2	0	50
SHREWSBURY	1884-87	7	5	2	0	71
STEEL	1886-88	4	3	1	0	75
READ	1888	1	1	0	0	100
GRACE	1888-99	13	8	3	2	69
STODDART	1893-98	8	3	4	1	44
MACLAREN	1897-09	22	4	11	7	34
P WARNER	1903-04	5	3	2	0	60
JACKSON	1905	5	2	0	3	70
FANE	1907-08	3	1	2	0	33
JONES	1908	2	0	2	0	0
DOUGLAS	1911-21	12	4	8	0	33
FRY	1912	3	1	0	2	67

In this first era England had a stronger record at home than they did in Australia. This is not surprising; in these early years it would often not be possible to take England's best XI on tour and the squads tended to be small (there were only 12 in the original 1877 tour) to maximise the profits per player. Naturally this meant that an illness or injury could have a big impact. England's success percentage at home was 61% and in Australia 46%. This benefitted Grace, who captained England in 10 Tests at home and in just three in Australia. Stanley Jackson only captained England in a single home series in 1905.

Some might think it odd that WG Grace was not appointed captain until his tenth Test match in 1888 and that he played under three captains beforehand, Lord Harris, AN Hornby and AG Steel. The fact is that WG, although an amateur, was not an amateur in the traditional mould. He did not go to public school nor to Oxford or Cambridge, because his family was not sufficiently wealthy. His position was unique in that his cricketing ability, his physique, his athleticism and his personality gave him a presence equal to that of any of the upper class amateur players; however he did not quite fit with the image of an England cricket captain in the minds of the Committee at Lords. This was probably not helped by the absence of certain qualities thought desirable in gentlemen, for example he made no secret of his disdain for reading and he showed himself to be a poor ambassador when he captained a tour to Australia in 1872-3.

However, the MCC certainly needed him. Their position as undisputed cricket authority with the right to set the rules of the game and to host the leading matches came under some challenge in the early to mid-1860s and their embracing of WG, whose cricketing talents were unequalled at the time may well have owed much to their determination to retain their role and to defend the club's status. He was elected a member at age 21, proposed by the Treasurer and seconded by the Secretary. Yet to be appointed captain was something else entirely and he was not appointed until the second Test of 1888, when the selectors were faced with a problem. England had just lost the opening Test to Australia at Lord's, only the second time England had lost a home Test and AG Steel, the captain, decided to stand down. No other traditional amateurs of real stature were available and finally the choice fell on WG.

Unsurprisingly he was a strong captain, confident in his own judgments. This was clearly illustrated by the third Test in 1896 when the match was delayed by rain and at the end of the second day of the three-day match England were 60-5 in their second innings, just 86 runs ahead. Grace inspected the pitch on the third morning, concluded that it was essential to get the Australians in quickly and so ordered England to get runs fast and to be all out in half an hour (in fact if necessary he could have declared; the rule allowing declarations had been introduced in 1889 and the first Test innings to be declared had been in 1893). England were duly all out for 84 and then bowled Australia out for 44 to win by 66 runs.

Like Grace, there is no doubt that Jackson was a strong captain. He was a natural leader with enormous self-confidence perhaps best expressed by EHD Sewell who wrote: "all that Jackson did on the cricket field he did so easily that it seemed the only thing to do". Jackson played his first Test against Australia in 1893 while still at Cambridge University and he was an immediate success. His military career (he served in the second Boer War) and other pressures restricted the time available for cricket and it was for this reason that he was unavailable for any of the Australian tours.

When WG retired after the first match of the home series against Australia in 1899, some might have expected Jackson to be appointed captain but in the event the honour went to Archie MacLaren and it was not until his final series in 1905 that Jackson became captain. Australia started as favourites for the series but under Jackson's captaincy England won two of the five games and were in the stronger position in each of the three drawn games. Just two wins out of five may not sound a tremendous achievement but it should be remembered that at the time Tests in England were limited to three days and with English weather it was not always possible to achieve a result. Jackson topped the batting averages for England and Australia combined with 492 runs at 70.28 raw average and also the combined bowling averages with 13 wickets at 15.46 apiece.

Of the other captains who led for five or more matches, both Plum Warner and Arthur Shrewsbury, with over 50% success rates, achieved 3-2 victories on tour to Australia and Shrewsbury also had two victories in England. Andrew Stoddart also enjoyed a 3-2 success on tour to Australia in 1894/95 but had two losses and one draw from his other three matches. A great sportsman who also captained England at rugby, Stoddart's 173 was crucial to England's win at Melbourne to take a 2-0 series lead in 1894/95 and remained the highest Ashes score by an England captain until Mike Denness made 188 in 1974/75.

Archie MacLaren captained England in 22 Ashes Tests, more than anyone else to date, leading them to four wins, seven draws and 11 defeats. He was a brilliant batsman but lacked the consistency at Test level to rank as highly in the averages (raw or adjusted) as one might have expected, this despite five wonderful centuries against Australia. His captaincy both on and off the field also displayed inconsistency and perhaps John Arlott's comments in Michael Down's biography of MacLaren published in 1981 sum it up: "It was MacLaren's tragedy that all his virtues bred their own faults. He was strong but inflexible, intelligent but intolerant, single-minded but humourless, impressive on the field, but often disappointingly petty off it." This of a man that Neville Cardus described as the "noblest Roman of them all". Certainly MacLaren inspired widely varying opinions among those who came into contact with him.

MacLaren went to public school at Harrow, following a few years behind Jackson, but his family did not have the financial resources to send him to university (he fared better than some of his younger siblings who were unable to go to public school). The family's position meant that he did not have the degree of financial security that certain other amateur players enjoyed and although he made himself available for overseas tours he worked at Harrow during the first part of the English season and was sometimes not available for county matches until early July. In 1895 in the first game of the season in which he played he made 424 against Somerset which was the record individual score in an English first class match until Brian Lara eclipsed it 99 years later. Michael Down writes: "Archie always had something of an inferiority complex because he could not really afford to live like a member of the landed gentry". One does wonder if this aggravated the faults to which Arlott referred.

* * *

2ND ERA ENGLAND CAPTAINS

The captains in Era 2 enjoyed mixed fortunes
as shown in the table below:

	SPAN	MATCHES	WON	LOST	DRAWN	%
DOUGLAS	1911-21	12	4	8	0	33
FRY	1912	3	1	0	2	67
TENNYSON	1921	3	0	1	2	33
GILLIGAN	1924-25	5	1	4	0	20
CARR	1926	4	0	0	4	50
CHAPMAN	1926-30	9	6	1	2	78
WHITE	1929	1	0	1	0	0
JARDINE	1932-33	5	4	1	0	80
WYATT	1930-34	5	1	2	2	40
WALTERS	1934	1	0	1	0	0
ALLEN	1936-37	5	2	3	0	40
HAMMOND	1938-47	8	1	3	4	38

Johnny Douglas, who had captained England to a 4-1 series victory in
Australia in 1911-12, was captain for the first seven Tests following
the First World War, all of which were won by Australia. Douglas
was a man of supreme fitness, who had won gold in the middleweight
boxing competition at the 1908 London Olympics. He would never
shirk any challenge, nor would his effort falter whatever the odds.
He was fortunate to be able to call on the bowling of Sydney Barnes
and the batting of Jack Hobbs in 1911/12 and equally unfortunate
that Australia were vastly superior in 1920/21 and 1921, due to the
bowling of Jack Gregory and Ted McDonald. Douglas was second
to Hobbs in the batting averages for 1920/21 as well as opening the
bowling in four of the five matches. Despite having been removed as
captain in favour of Lionel Tennyson following the first two Tests
of the 1921 series, Douglas showed his continued commitment with
three wickets in Australia's first innings and a top score of 75 in
England's first innings which enabled them to save the follow on,

though ultimately not the match. This was the last in a series of eight successive defeats, the final two matches of that series being drawn.

After the unsuccessful 1924/25 tour led by Arthur Gilligan and four drawn matches under Arthur Carr in 1926, Percy Chapman was appointed for the last match at the Oval. Chapman was the only truly successful England captain in Era 2, other than Douglas Jardine. His captaincy began with England's first win against Australia since the First World War, thanks to the batting of Jack Hobbs and Herbert Sutcliffe in the second innings followed by the bowling of Wilfred Rhodes (who had been recalled, aged 48). On the tour to Australia in 1928/29, Chapman led one of the strongest England sides in history. They won the first four games before losing the last from which Chapman was absent with flu.

In 1930, Don Bradman scored his record series aggregate of 974 and he was strongly supported by Bill Woodfull, Bill Ponsford and Stan McCabe. Yet England, still led by Chapman, were on level terms at one Test apiece going into the fifth and final match of the series. The England selectors dropped Chapman for that decisive match in a bid to strengthen the middle order batting, and England lost. Chapman led England on the following winter tour of South Africa after which Douglas Jardine took over. As a captain Chapman inspired his team through his unsurpassed fielding, his cheerful confidence and his personal charm. Despite being a fine batsman he was inevitably eclipsed by Hobbs, Sutcliffe and Hammond. However, to captain England to six wins and two draws in nine Ashes Tests when Bradman was on the opposing side in seven of them is not a bad record.

Douglas Jardine's only Ashes captaincy was on the notorious Bodyline tour. He was a fine batsman whose overall Test match average was 48, although just 31.76 against Australia, and he displayed strong leadership skills and tactical acumen. However, his resolution and determination to succeed seem to have been at the expense of a normal level of sensitivity to his actions. This is clear from the fact that Bodyline did not command the universal agreement of the English team (for example, Gubby Allen refused to bowl the infamous leg theory and some others were uneasy). However, it should be said that Jardine considered the tactics fair and was backed by the MCC throughout the tour, although they were too far away to appreciate the strength of feeling in Australia.

Bob Wyatt, who replaced Chapman as skipper in the last match of the 1930 series, took over from Jardine for 1934, although he missed the first match due to a fractured thumb. He and Gubby Allen, who led the 1936/37 tour, both had 40% records.

Wally Hammond changed from being a professional to an amateur in order to have the chance to captain England, which he did for the four matches of the 1938 series. He also captained England after the War, for the first four Tests of the 1946/47 series, missing the final match because of fibrositis. As captain Hammond was considered to have done a strong job in 1938 but much less so in 1946/47. He was described as "sagacious and inspiring" for his leadership in 1938, although some felt that in a couple of the matches he could have made greater use of his spin bowling. More generally, his shyness and modesty meant that he did not offer the outgoing encouragement to the younger players which might have been expected from him. In 1946/47 these problems were exacerbated by his ill health and perhaps this and the high priority given to building cricket goodwill in the aftermath of the war diluted the resolve which was needed to challenge the more determined Australians.

***

3RD ERA ENGLAND CAPTAINS

Era 3 was not an easy time for England,
as shown by the following figures:

	SPAN	MATCHES	WON	LOST	DRAWN	%
HAMMOND	1938-47	8	1	3	4	38
YARDLEY	1947-48	6	0	5	1	8
BROWN	1950-51	5	1	4	0	20
HUTTON	1953-55	10	4	1	5	65
MAY	1956-61	13	3	6	4	38
COWDREY	1961-68	6	1	2	3	42
DEXTER	1962-64	10	1	2	7	45
M SMITH	1965-66	5	1	1	3	50
GRAVENEY	1968	1	0	0	1	50
ILLINGWORTH	1970-72	11	4	2	5	59
DENNESS	1974-75	6	1	4	1	25
J EDRICH	1975	1	0	1	0	0
GREIG	1975-77	4	0	1	3	38

It was not until the 15th Test after World War Two at the end of
the 1950/51 series, with England captained by Freddie Brown and
Bradman retired, that England recorded their first victory.

Len Hutton, England's first professional captain since 1887, took
the helm for Coronation year in 1953. His success record of 65% was
the strongest in Era 3 and in his two Ashes series as captain he became
the first English captain to regain the Ashes and then to defend them
successfully. Hutton was described by AA Thomson, in his book,
Hutton and Washbrook, as steadfast under continual pressure, strong
in his determination to build an England XI capable of beating all
Test countries and a man of complete integrity. Appointed in 1952,
he had an amateur rival in David Sheppard, put forward by those who
believed that the England captain should not be a professional, but
with changing times the amateur/professional distinction had virtually
become irrelevant (it was finally abolished altogether in 1962). Hutton's

experience and status at the time gave him the stronger claim for the role. As a man and captain he was introspective and he worried considerably and often visibly. His burdens often included a disproportionate responsibility for England's batting, certainly until England's leading younger batsmen in the shape of Peter May and Colin Cowdrey began to cement their own reputations.

May captained England to victory in the 1956 series thanks largely to Jim Laker's magnificent performance and as England's strongest batsman he very much led from the front. However, May's overall captaincy record suffered from the series losses in 1958/59 and 1961. Test cricket had entered that dull period of the 1950s and 1960s when there seemed to be fewer truly inspirational players and the game seemed less entertaining. May was handicapped at times by illness and as an undemonstrative captain lacked the inspirational skills possessed by the likes of Grace and Chapman but he could perhaps not have been expected to deliver more with the players available at the time.

Ted Dexter was more outgoing and was a deep-thinking captain, although he did make mistakes not least at Headingley in 1964. His decision to take the new ball at a time when England's spinners were on top, resulted in Australia moving from 178 for 7 to 389 all out and helped them to a seven-wicket win in the only match of the series to achieve a result. As an aggressive stroke-playing batsman he had no equal at the time and was one of few batsmen in Ashes history who could completely change a game in the space of half an hour. However, this was rarely enough to inspire his team mates to rise out of the sluggishness that tarnished many games during that period. As a consequence, England drew seven of the 10 Ashes matches in which he captained them, losing one series and drawing another in the process.

Despite being three years older than Dexter, Cowdrey followed him into the role of Ashes captain in 1968 when he was 36. He was the perfect gentleman and most elegant of batsmen and, although he lacked the toughness required to become the most successful of captains, his courage as a cricketer was never in doubt. A prime example was his willingness to fly out to join England's Ashes tour of 1974/75, after an absence of more than four years from Test cricket, as cover for Dennis Amiss and John Edrich, both of whom had had their hands broken during the first Test. Four days after his arrival, and just a couple of weeks short of his 42nd birthday, Cowdrey was batting at number 3 in the second Test and facing Dennis Lillee and Jeff Thomson. Similarly, 12 years earlier he had returned to the crease with a broken arm, when England were nine wickets down in the Lord's Test against the West Indies in 1963.

Mike Smith was preferred to Cowdrey in 1965/66 and in his personable way managed to inject a lighter spirit into the team. For 1970/71 Cowdrey was the favoured choice of many critics, however the selectors chose Ray Illingworth, a robust, down-to-earth York-shireman. Illingworth was prepared to take tough decisions, refusing to enforce the follow on at Adelaide when the pace bowlers were too tired and taking his team off the field at Sydney after a crowd demonstration against John Snow's bowling. Despite hostility from the critics during the 1970/71 tour, he enjoyed the players' trust throughout, winning the series. England retained the Ashes thanks to a 2-2 result in 1972, giving him a success rate of 59% and placing him second to Len Hutton on 65%.

Mike Denness was unlucky to lead a team which ran into Lillee and Thomson at their peak and as a one-series captain he was never going to be able to show a high success rate. Tony Greig's captaincy was also short lived, because of his association with Kerry Packer's World Series Cricket.

***

The first five years of Era 4 gave one of those graphic illustrations which occur every few decades of just how important the choice of captain can be, and that it may not be the right thing to have the strongest, most inspirational player as captain. Mike Brearley was appointed captain for the home Ashes series in 1977, which England won 3-0 (helped in part by the controversy over the forthcoming WSC). Ian Botham made his England debut in the third Test, taking five wickets in Australia's first innings before achieving the same in the following match. Brearley opened the batting throughout, making 50 only once and averaging less than 30. In the 1978/79 series against an Australian side weakened by the defections to Kerry Packer's WSC, Brearley, averaging less than 20 with the bat, led England to a 5-1 win. Christopher Martin Jenkins in his *Who's Who of Test Cricketers*, wrote of Brearley: "Clear thinking, calmness under pressure and decisiveness were his major qualities on the field, fair mindedness and consideration for others the main ones off it. It was all the more remarkable that he retained the complete faith of his team mates despite failing to justify a place as a top England batsman." Rodney Hogg famously described Brearley as having a "degree in People" and this shows in the 69% success rate England achieved under his leadership.

4TH ERA ENGLAND CAPTAINS

	SPAN	MATCHES	WON	LOST	DRAWN	%
BREARLEY	1977-81	18	11	4	3	69
BOTHAM	1980-81	3	0	1	2	33
WILLIS	1982-83	5	1	2	2	40
GOWER	1985-89	12	3	5	4	42
GATTING	1986-88	6	2	1	3	58
LAMB	1990	1	0	1	0	0
GOOCH	1990-93	8	0	5	3	19
ATHERTON	1993-01	15	4	9	2	33
A STEWART	1998-99	5	1	3	1	30

However England lost 3-0 to Australia in the non-Ashes series of 1979/80 which was arranged hurriedly (alongside a three-match series between Australia and the West Indies) to recognise the re-entry to Test cricket of the WSC players, in particular the many Australians, after the agreement reached between Kerry Packer and the cricket authorities. After this series, in which Brearley averaged a slightly better 34 with the bat, he stood down from the captaincy in favour of Botham, and lost his place in the side, for the 1980 West Indies series. In 1981, under Botham, England lost the first Test and drew the second and the captain was not enjoying his role, finding that it was affecting his batting and bowling. Following a "pair" in the drawn second Test, Botham resigned the captaincy. Brearley, by then aged 39, was recalled to the team and reinstated as captain. The rest is, as they say, history. England won the next three Tests and the series largely due to the efforts of Botham, now unburdened by the captaincy.

England's next captains David Gower and Mike Gatting enjoyed brief success in the mid-1980s and at 58% Gatting had a strong success rate. However, both players tend to be remembered more for their batting successes than accomplishments as captains. Gower was dropped as captain after England lost 5-0 to West Indies in 1985/6 though he was restored later in the decade. From the late-1980s through to the end of the 1990s, there was a long period where the England captaincy was unsettled, which only compounded Australia's dominance. Gooch (eight Tests), Atherton (15) and Stewart (five) couldn't be faulted for commitment but none could deliver the results that England needed.

* * *

The Australian dominance continued in 2001 and 2002/03 through no fault of England's new captain Nasser Hussain. However, by 2005 the tide had turned and England felt more confident. The success of captains since then has owed much to the team's preparation and the off-field work of the coaches, which is driven partly by the need for higher levels of fitness and training in the one-day game. As you can see from the table below, Michael Vaughan and Andrew Strauss achieved strong results as did Alastair Cook in his first series as captain in 2013. The 2013/14 series however was a disaster for England and seemed to show up limitations in Cook's captaincy, particularly in the high level of caution he displayed when a more active style might have brought better returns. Under Joe Root, England have so far lost a series in Australia and drawn one in England and supporters will be hoping for a strong focus on the five-day game as well as T20 and ODIs to improve for the next series.

CURRENT ERA ENGLAND CAPTAINS

	SPAN	MATCHES	WON	LOST	DRAWN	%
HUSSAIN	2001-03	8	2	6	0	25
VAUGHAN	2005	5	2	1	2	60
FLINTOFF	2006-07	5	0	5	0	0
STRAUSS	2009-11	10	5	2	3	65
COOK	2013-15	15	6	7	2	47
ROOT	2017-	10	2	6	2	30

Andrew Flintoff captained a side which lost 5-0 in 2006/07 demonstrating, as with Botham, that the team's most exciting and inspirational player is not always the right choice for captain. He made mistakes most notably by declaring too early in the second test at Adelaide but a greater factor was probably that, during the tour, the England preparation and off field management, which had thrived under Duncan Fletcher for the previous five years failed to deliver. An equally large factor was the combined efforts of Glenn McGrath, Shane Warne, Adam Gilchrist, Justin Langer and Matthew Hayden in their last Ashes series.

Between 2006/07 and 2009 England again experimented unsuccessfully with the policy of choosing an exciting inspirational player as captain in Kevin Pietersen. However, Pietersen did not captain an Ashes Test and by the start of the 2009 series not only was Strauss in place as the new captain, but so too was a new management team headed by the ex-Zimbabwe batsman Andy Flower.

Strauss proved a highly successful captain leading England to victory in 2009 and 2010/11 and initially Alistair Cook continued this with a 3-0 series win in 2013 before a 5-0 loss in 2013/14. The off-field training, development and selection framework established by Andy Flower clearly played a large part in England's success between 2009 and 2013 but the sharp reversal in the 2013/14 series resulted in the replacement of Flower by Peter Moores. It was Moores's second term in the role, after he had held it briefly from 2007 to 2009 and this too was short lived and did not include an Ashes series. Strauss himself was appointed to the position of director of cricket prior to the 2015 series and replaced Moores with Australian coach Trevor Bayliss. The 2015 series ended in a 3-2 series win for England in Cook's third series as captain.

Cook retired as captain after the 2015 series but his appetite for playing was undiminished and he continued as first choice opening batsman until his retirement from Test cricket at the end of the series against India in 2018. Joe Root took over as captain and with his confident, composed approach seems well suited in temperament for the role though there is a feeling in some quarters that he should be more pro-active and inspirational. Certainly, with a 4-0 series loss in Australia in 2017/18 and a drawn series in England in 2019 he will feel a strong duty to improve the team's performance. The right off-field support in selection and coaching is also of major importance. In Australia in 2017/18 England failed to assemble a seam attack with genuine pace and lacked a real spinner and in 2019 the onlooker might wonder if the strong focus on the one-day game in the run up to the World Cup affected Ashes preparation.

This section should really end with an opinion on who was England's greatest captain. It's certainly not possible to do this just by looking at success percentages. As we've said any captain is far too dependent on the core abilities of the rest of his team for those to be a sufficient measure. Account must also be taken of the strength of the opposing teams, the number of games captained (if there are too few too much can be influenced by chance), proportion of games played home and away and so on.

The captains who, to me do stand out include Grace for his confidence and self-belief, Chapman for his out-going personality, motivation and effectiveness at a time when Bradman was on the other side and Hutton for his grit and determination in winning a series at home and a series away at a time when much of the batting was dependent on him. But we must also consider Illingworth for his confounding of the critics and refusal to be fazed by events, Brearley for his insight and motivational qualities and Strauss for his calm thoughtful approach and courage to act on it (putting Australia in to bat twice in 2010/11). Most had success percentages in the 60s with

Illingworth just below at 59 and Chapman above at 78.

I thought it might be interesting to compare the batting performances of Grace, Hutton and Strauss (all opening batsmen) as captain with their batting performances as non-captain. Both Grace (42.12 versus 63.12) and Hutton (45.96 versus 59.04) have significantly lower adjusted batting averages when captain whilst Strauss, albeit with much lower averages than Grace and Hutton has a significantly higher batting average when captain (41.59 versus 29.81). It's open to debate how much this tells us. Grace was 40 years of age when he became captain so perhaps it's not surprising if his batting was on the wane, while Hutton turned 37 within a week of his first Ashes Test as captain. Strauss took command of his first Ashes Test at a relatively sprightly 32.

Any choice here is highly subjective. Rather than anoint a particular individual I prefer to say that purely as captains, Strauss, Brearley and Chapman from different eras and showing different, but arguably equally effective, qualities in leadership were England's top captains in Ashes Tests with Illingworth not far behind. Others such as Grace and Hutton were very highly effective captains but perhaps owed more to their stature as great batsmen and their great cricket experience.

AUSTRALIA

Compared to the 53 captains used by England in Ashes matches, Australia have used just 41, 14 of whom were used during Era 1 prior to World War One. Six of these captained for three or fewer matches and so the success percentages cannot be considered meaningful.

The table shows the figures:

TABLE OVERLEAF

1ST ERA AUSTRALIAN CAPTAINS

	SPAN	MATCHES	WON	LOST	DRAWN	%
D GREGORY	1877-79	3	2	1	0	67
MURDOCH	1880-90	16	5	7	4	44
HORAN	1885	2	0	2	0	0
MASSIE	1885	1	1	0	0	100
BLACKHAM	1885-94	8	3	3	2	50
SCOTT	1886	3	0	3	0	0
MCDONNELL	1887-88	6	1	5	0	17
GIFFEN	1894-95	4	2	2	0	50
TROTT	1896-98	8	5	3	0	63
J DARLING	1899-05	18	5	4	9	53
TRUMBLE	1902	2	2	0	0	100
NOBLE	1903-09	15	8	5	2	60
HILL	1911-12	5	1	4	0	20
S GREGORY	1912	3	0	1	2	33

Prior to September 1892 when the short-lived Australasian Cricket Council (ACC) was formed, Test matches in Australia were run by the host state. The first state to host a series was Victoria, with matches being held in Melbourne. New South Wales followed, with the first Test at Sydney being played in March 1882 and South Australia hosted its first Test at Adelaide played in December 1884. (Brisbane and Perth followed much later.) The captain was only chosen after the team was selected and he was chosen by the players themselves. Given the lack of a consistent selection body and the frequent disputes between the players and the host state over financial terms, the team which played was not always Australia's best. The chaos this could produce reached its peak in the five-match series in 1884/85 when Australia changed their captain after each Test, reappointing one of the previous captains for the final Test, and used nine debutants in the team for the second Test.

These changes of captaincy, but most particularly in playing personnel, had a negative impact on Australian performance over this period. Billy Murdoch, who had captained many of the early matches, returned to the role in 1890 only to lose two matches, leaving him with a success rate of 44% from his 16 matches as captain. He was replaced by Jack Blackham, who had played in the first test in 1877 and another 27 following that, but had captained Australia only once. Now 37 years of age, Blackham would keep the role for the remaining seven matches of his Test career, covering the 1891/92 series, which Australia won 2-1, and the 1893 series in England, which was lost 1-0. In the end Blackham was forced to retire after the first Test of the home series in 1894/95 because of long term damage to his thumb from wicketkeeping.

George Giffen, whom we discussed in Chapter 9, then took on the role with Australia winning two and losing two of the remaining four Tests in the series. Giffen was the leading Australian player of his time and would have played more than the 31 tests which he did against England but for various disputes, including some over pay, and also his refusal on occasions to play if his brother Walter was not selected. By the time he was appointed captain, he was 35 years old and in the words of Malcom Knox, "He was not a natural Test captain with his unwillingness to delegate and his bloody-minded pursuit of principle over common sense", Perhaps because of these failings, the players chose Harry Trott to captain the side on the 1896 tour of England, although Giffen played in all three Tests.

Wisden wrote of Trott: "Blessed with a humour that nothing could ruffle, Harry Trott was always master both of himself and his team, whatever the position of the game". He had a real captain's instinct for the game being frequently successful in following his own hunches on bowling changes. As a batsman his one Ashes century, 143 at Lord's in 1896, facilitated a partnership of 221 with Syd Gregory and made a match out of what could have been a rout of Australia, who had been bowled out for 53 in their first innings. The 4-1 series win in Australia in 1897/98 gives Trott a strong overall success rate of 63%. Sadly his health deteriorated and he played no more Test cricket.

Joe Darling took over for the 1899 tour and, apart from two games captained by Hugh Trumble in 1901/02, he shared the captaincy with Monty Noble over the following seven series. Darling had a success rate of 53% from 18 games, while Noble had a success rate of 60%

from 15 games. Clem Hill and Syd Gregory each captained a series to end the era before WW1.

Darling was a strong captain much respected by his players. The series victory in 1899 saw him become the first Australian captain to win a series in England since the 1882 Test at the Oval that led to the creation of the Ashes, effectively making it the first Ashes series win for Australia in England. Not beaten in a series until 1905, Darling's pinnacle was the 2-1 victory in England in 1902. The Australian team, called "a somewhat forlorn and dispirited set of cricketers" by Wisden on their arrival in England, were dismissed for just 36 in the first Test, their lowest ever Test score but, having followed on 340 runs behind, were saved by the rain at 46/2 in the second innings. The second Test was also a washout but Australia won the third and fourth Tests, the latter by just three runs, to retain the Ashes. Darling, whose form with the bat collapsed, made himself unavailable for the 1903/04 series but returned to captain the side in his final Test series in 1905 in England.

By 1900 the ACC had been disbanded, to be remembered as a failed attempt by the cricket associations to take control over Australian tours to England and England tours to Australia. In 1905 a new body, The Australian Board of Control of International Cricket, was formed to oversee all the Australian national representative cricket sides. In time this body would take over full control of tour finances and organisation and, from 1909, responsibility for appointing the captain[9].

Monty Noble who had captained the 1903/04 home series in Darling's absence took over the captaincy for the 1907/08 home series and continued for the England tour in 1909 after which he retired. Series wins of 4-1 in 1907/08 and 2-1 in 1909 gave him a success percentage of 60. Another strong captain he believed in true sportsmanship and off-the-field discipline.

***

[9]   *The forerunner of Cricket Australia, it was known as the Australian Cricket Board from 1973, before acquiring its current name in 2003.*

2ND ERA AUSTRALIAN CAPTAINS

The Era 2 table is:

	SPAN	MATCHES	WON	LOST	DRAWN	%
ARMSTRONG	1920-21	10	8	0	2	90
COLLINS	1924-26	8	4	2	2	63
BARDSLEY	1926	2	0	0	2	50
RYDER	1928-29	5	1	4	0	20
WOODFULL	1930-34	15	5	6	4	47
BRADMAN	1936-48	19	11	3	5	71

Warwick Armstrong, who played in 32 Tests before World War One, was appointed captain at the age of 41 for the first post-war series against England, which was played in Australia in 1920/21. Known for his all-round skills and experience (including his further ten matches as captain, he would finish with 2,172 runs and 74 wickets against England) , Armstrong did not have the tactical skills of Noble but was fortunate enough to be in command of one of the strongest sides in Australian history. He had a huge physical presence weighing in at an unhealthy 22 stone, but this did not stop him from achieving a success rate of 90%, only bettered by Hugh Massie, Hugh Trumble and Neil Harvey, none of whom captained more than twice.

Herbie Collins captained for the home series in 1924/25, and in England for 1926 except for two games when he was ill. His approach to captaincy was to think through the day's events on his own and to study his opponents' weaknesses. As the senior Australian batsman as well as captain, he took the brunt of Maurice Tate's hostile bowling in the first Test of 1924/25, protecting his partner Bill Ponsford who was making his debut and thus ensuring Australia had a strong start to the series which they went on to win 4-1. In 1926 the series was lost 1-0, the last Test, played on a timeless basis being the only one to produce a result.

Jack Ryder, with a 20% record from his one series in charge in 1928/29 had the misfortune to be captain at the one point in the inter-war years when England's strength was clearly greater than Australia's.

Bill Woodfull was captain for three Ashes, the tours to England in 1930 and 1934 and the Bodyline series in 1932/33. Bradman's batting took Australia to 2-1 series wins in each series in England but the Bodyline series was lost 4-1. Woodfull was a teetotal captain, whose qualities were perhaps best summarised by Ray Robinson when he wrote: "the kernel of Woodfull's captaincy was the way he got the utmost from each man. Their esteem was their response to his personal qualities of common sense, straightforwardness, tolerance, consideration and unselfish service to his side". To these qualities should be added an unfailing courage which was most noticeable throughout the Bodyline tour. The tension in that series came to a head in the third Test at Adelaide after Bert Oldfield's skull had been fractured and Woodfull had also been injured by a delivery from Larwood, although it should be noted that neither delivery was the fast, leg theory which was dubbed Bodyline. When Pelham Warner, England's tour manager, went to the Australian changing room at the end of the day's play, Woodfull, who was receiving treatment, said: "I don't want to see you, Mr Warner. There are two teams out there on the oval. One is playing cricket, the other is not. This game is too good to be spoilt. It is time some people got out of it". Australia lost the Adelaide Test by 338 runs, being bowled out for 193 in their second innings. However, Woodfull played one of his greatest innings, carrying his bat and ending on 73 not out.

The 4-1 loss in the Bodyline series gives Woodfull an overall success rate as captain of just 47% but this surely underrates him. He remains to date the only Australian captain to have regained the Ashes twice, in 1930 and 1934 (on both occasions the victory was clinched on 22 August, his birthday)[10]. In November 1934 Woodfull was offered a knighthood for services to cricket but he declined, considering his work as a maths teacher, to be more important. However, in 1963 he was pleased to accept an OBE for services to education.

There is a clear consensus that Bradman is the greatest ever batsman.

---

[10]   It should perhaps be said that if the 1979/80 series had been accorded Ashes status, Greg Chappell would also have regained the Ashes twice.

Equally there is a consensus that he was not a born leader, and he certainly did not seek the captaincy of Australia. In fact he wasn't captain of his state side in the Sheffield Shield until 1935 when he joined South Australia having moved from his home state of New South Wales to join a firm of stockbrokers in Adelaide. However, given the widely held belief in Australian cricket that the captain should be the strongest batsman, there was perhaps an inevitability that Bradman would eventually lead his country. A serious bout of appendicitis at the end of the 1934 England tour and the need to reach agreement with the Board of Control over his various commercial agreements delayed his appointment and he didn't take over as captain until the 1936/37 series against England. The first two Tests were lost to an England side which had much the better luck with pitch conditions for batting and Bradman did not do well himself with the bat making two ducks and scoring just 120 runs in four completed innings.

A corner was turned in the third Test at Melbourne in difficult conditions. After batting first, Bradman declared at 200 for 9 to put England in on a rain-affected wicket. Belatedly perhaps Gubby Allen returned the compliment and declared England's innings closed at 76 for 9 towards the end of the day. Bradman then sent in tail-enders Bill O'Reilly, Chuck Fleetwood-Smith and Frank Ward in the first three batting positions to protect the top order (himself included) from the 35 minutes of difficult batting that evening. Just one wicket was lost and following a rain-free rest day Bradman made 270 in an Australian second innings total of 564 to set up victory by 365 runs. Victories followed in the next two Tests, including a further double century and another innings of more than 150 from Bradman. The series in England in 1938 was drawn 1-1 but the two post-war series in 1946/47 and 1948 featured two of the strongest Australian sides in history and were won by 3-0 and 4-0 giving Bradman a success rate overall of 71%.

How effective was Bradman as a captain? One has to look at the position in the pre-war and post-war years separately. Bill O'Reilly quoted in Malcolm Knox's book described Bradman as "a teetotaller, ambitious, conservative and meticulous" (in contrast to his own more gregarious nature). Malcom Knox writes "He could not help his personality. The greatest captains can transcend these differences and inspire their men nonetheless. Woodfull was also an ambitious, meticulous teetotaller but his Irish Catholic teammates would have died for him. There was something about Bradman that some players in the 1930s didn't like. They respected him and knew he was the best thing they had going for them, but they didn't love him and in the final analysis of the Australian captaincy, the very best have engendered a kind of love". However, after the war it was different. Bradman enjoyed such an elevated status and the Australian side such overall superiority that no such tensions ever materialised.

***

3RD ERA AUSTRALIAN CAPTAINS

The Era 3 table is:

	SPAN	MATCHES	WON	LOST	DRAWN	%
BRADMAN	1936-48	19	11	3	5	71
HASSETT	1950-53	10	4	2	4	60
JOHNSON	1954-56	9	2	4	3	39
MORRIS	1954	1	0	1	0	0
BENAUD	1958-63	14	6	2	6	64
HARVEY	1961	1	1	0	0	100
SIMPSON	1964-66	8	2	0	6	63
BOOTH	1965-66	2	0	1	1	25
LAWRY	1968-71	9	1	2	6	44
JARMAN	1968	1	0	0	1	50
I CHAPPELL	1971-75	16	7	4	5	59
G CHAPPELL	1977-83	15	6	4	5	57

Lindsay Hassett had been Bradman's vice-captain for the second post-war series in 1948 and took over the captaincy after Bradman's retirement. By the time of England's tour to Australia in 1950/51 Hassett was already well established, having led the team for their tour to South Africa the previous year. Managing to combine sportsmanship and light-heartedness with a firm authority, he was prepared to back his judgement and carry out apparently unusual actions when needed such as declaring at 32-7 at Brisbane to catch England for a second time on the unplayable wicket. Australia won the series 4-1 but lost in England 1-0 in 1953 in the second of Hassett's two series as Ashes captain giving him an overall success rate of 60%.

Dispensing with the policy of choosing a batsman as captain the Australian Board then appointed Ian Johnson, rather than Neil Harvey or Keith Miller. Both Ashes series for which Johnson captained were lost, however his 39% success rate against England is counterbalanced to some extent by successes on three other overseas tours.

Richie Benaud was captain for the 1958/59, 1961 and 1962/63 series. In many cases the success rates for captains reflect the relative strengths of the sides as much as the strength of the captain. Occasionally though there are exceptions and Benaud does seem to have been one of these. He had an outgoing personality and led from the front and took various initiatives to strengthen team morale which were ahead of their time, such as team-only dinners on the eve of Test matches. England's 1958/59 touring side were considered favourites but were soundly beaten 4-0 and then at a time when there was no clear superiority of either side, Benaud led the team to a 2-1 series win in England in 1961 and a 1-1 draw in 1962/63, culminating in an overall success rate of 64%.

Bob Simpson replaced Benaud and captained Australia for the 1964 and 1965/66 series. (Brian Booth captained for two matches in the latter series, when Simpson was first injured and then fell ill with chickenpox). Uncompromising in his pursuit of Ashes success, Simpson's own batting and his opening partnership with Bill Lawry were often key factors. His 311 at Old Trafford in 1964 (his first Test century in his 29th test) made it impossible for England to win and so ensured Australia retained the Ashes. His 225 at Adelaide in 1965/66 helped Australia win by an innings, squaring the series after they had gone one down while Simpson was ill. Two wins and six draws from his eight matches gave him a 63% success rate when England seemed to be a little stronger than Australia on paper and paints a picture of another strong Australian captain.

Lawry captained for the 1968 series, except for one game when he was injured, and for the first five of the six-Test home series in 1970/71 after which he was sacked in favour of Ian Chappell. If Simpson was uncompromising, Lawry took matters to an altogether new level. The key match in the 1968 series was the fourth, Australia having won the first and England being unable to press home their advantages in the second and third because of the weather. Lawry was injured and unable to play, but it is generally accepted that the defensive tactics adopted to secure a draw by Barry Jarman, Lawry's vice-captain were at the behest of the skipper. England won the final Test to square the series but Australia retained the Ashes.

In the first two matches of the 1970/71 series Lawry cemented his reputation as a captain whose first priority was to avoid losing, with slow scoring personal batting performances in the second innings of each game. England secured a win in the third Test but two more draws followed with Lawry continuing with his defensive approach both at the crease and as captain. By now the Australian Board had had enough and took the unprecedented step of sacking their captain during a Test series.

Ian Chappell took over for the final match, the first of 16 Ashes Tests in which he captained Australia. Chappell started boldly, putting England in to bat in his first Test as captain and being justified by England's total of 184, although Australia ultimately lost the game. From then on he captained Australia against England in three series drawing the first and then, as the pace bowling advantage moved from England to Australia, winning the next two. His approach to captaincy is well illustrated by journalist Gideon Haigh writing in *The Times*: "Ian Chappell fashioned an Australian team in his own image between 1971 and 1975: aggressive, resourceful and insouciant". He led his players by example, rather than by enforcing strict discipline, leading Mike Brearley to write: "Ian Chappell's Australia team exuded belligerence".

Chappell's determined approach to batting and fielding was a fine example to his team, however there were sometimes lapses in other areas. Occasional bursts of ill temper in the field created incidents and it is said that he was one of the players responsible for the growth of sledging. Throughout his career he fought for players' welfare and financial rewards. His belief that he had failed to achieve a fair deal for his team in his discussions with the Australian Board in the mid-1970s resulted in his resigning the captaincy after the series in England in 1975 and his subsequent association with Kerry Packer enabled Packer to launch his World Series Cricket successfully.

Chappell's brother Greg took over, his first match as captain against England being the Centenary Test in 1977 and he captained the team in 15 Ashes Tests until the end of the 1982/83 series. With a success rate of 59% for Ian and 57% for Greg, the brothers were successful captains.

***

News of Kerry Packer's WSC broke on the eve of the 1977 Ashes series, Greg Chappell's first series in charge. This had a bad psychological effect on the Australians. Thirteen of the touring party of 18, including Greg himself, were signed up with Packer. The series was lost 3-0 and it's not likely that any captain could, in the circumstances, have given the team the leadership and inspiration needed.

4TH ERA AUSTRALIAN CAPTAINS

	SPAN	MATCHES	WON	LOST	DRAWN	%
G CHAPPELL	1977-83	15	6	4	5	57
YALLOP	1978-79	6	1	5	0	17
HUGHES	1981	6	1	3	2	33
BORDER	1985-93	29	13	6	10	62
TAYLOR	1994-99	16	9	4	3	66

The Australian Board refused to consider any of the Packer rebels for Test matches during the time of the WSC and so a new captain and an almost completely new team was required. Bob Simpson was recalled at age 41 to captain the series against India and the West Indies but Graham Yallop was appointed for the six-match home series against England in 1978/79. Although a fine attacking batsman who topped the run aggregate for Australia in the series with two hundreds, Yallop's inward looking nature did not make him a natural leader. Over-attacking fields and on-field disputes with Rodney Hogg, his main strike bowler, seemed to be clumsy attempts to exert authority. However it wasn't Yallop's fault that the absence of the WSC players gave England a clear superiority which was reflected in the 5-1 series loss.

After a compromise was reached between the Australian Board and the WSC, the rebel players returned for the three match series in 1979/80. It was an unusual series being interspersed with Tests between Australia and the West Indies and it did not have Ashes status. Greg Chappell was reappointed captain and the series was won 3-0. However the strain from the sheer volume of cricket he had played over the years was becoming too much. This culminated in a request to his brother Trevor to bowl underarm in an ODI to prevent Australia's opponents New Zealand having the chance to hit a six and tie the match. Greg Chappell needed a rest and wasn't available for the tour to England in 1981 which was captained by Kim Hughes.

Hughes was not a particularly effective captain and also had a poor tour with the bat, although in fairness to him the 3-1 loss said more about England's strong performance inspired by Ian Botham, than Australia's weakness.

Greg Chappell returned as captain for the 1982/83 series which was duly won 2-1. In his book *The Complete Who's Who of Test Cricketers*, CMJ says of Greg in 1977, "He was a less successful motivator of men than his brother Ian, but it is perhaps unfair to lay much of the blame for Australia's failures against England at the door of their captain, who scored most runs for his team (371 at 41.22) including a memorable century against the tide of English success at Old Trafford and who by then had decided to join most of his fellows in Kerry Packer's World series cricket" This is surely the point; Greg was primarily a batsman rather than a captain and he had the misfortune to have the captaincy thrust on him in turbulent times. Nevertheless in pure numbers his success rate of 57% is creditable.

Allan Border took over the captaincy for the 1985 tour to England and by the time he passed the captaincy on to Mark Taylor had captained Australia in a record 29 matches against England. The first two series were lost as Australia were rebuilding their side and England were at a cyclical peak with David Gower and Botham in their pomp and a generally strong batting line up. Border was Australia's leading run scorer in 1985 with 597 runs at 66.33 and second behind Dean Jones in 1986/87 with 473 at 52.55.

Bob Simpson was appointed permanent coach to the side, a position which had not previously existed and together with Border, they built a harder and more aggressive team. This was noticeable in the 1989 series which Australia won 4-0 and in the 3-0 and 4-1 series victories which followed in 1990/91 and 1993. Malcolm Knox believed that Border even as an experienced captain saw himself as a student of captaincy, writing: "He was the most "normal" individual to be a captain and it was that very unpretentiousness that won him the kind of love from his players that Ian Chappell and Richie Benaud had won for their charisma". By the time Border handed the captaincy to Taylor, Australia's dominance over England was complete.

Several factors contributed to the calm authority that Taylor projected and the resulting respect he gained from his players. It was not only his all-round cricket ability; there was also the status he achieved from his 839 run aggregate in the 1989 series and not least the dominance of Australia. All three series under his captaincy were won and no-one who captained as many times as he did had a greater success record than his 66% except Bradman.

***

CURRENT ERA AUSTRALIAN CAPTAINS

The Era 5 table is:

	SPAN	MATCHES	WON	LOST	DRAWN	%
S WAUGH	2001-03	9	8	1	0	89
GILCHRIST	2001	1	0	1	0	0
PONTING	2005-10	19	8	6	5	55
CLARKE	2011-15	16	7	7	2	50
S SMITH	2017-18	5	4	0	1	90
PAINE	2019-	5	2	2	1	50

Both series in which Taylor's successor Steve Waugh captained were won 4-1 and Waugh was absent injured in the lost game in 2001. Not content just to ride the wave of success Australia enjoyed, Waugh brought in John Buchanan as cricket coach to help him build a new focused, confident approach. Among players who captained Australia more than twice Waugh's success rate of 89% is only beaten by Warwick Armstrong's 90% and now by Steve Smith's 90% from his one series as captain at home in 2017/18.

Ricky Ponting took over at a time when England and Australia were more finely balanced. He led from the front as his country's top batsman and his fighting qualities were never in doubt. Although he lost three series out of four in which he was captain (Clarke took over for the last match of the 2010/11 series when Ponting was injured), he still won more games than he lost.

Michael Clarke, who retired following the 2015 series, embodied the same qualities as Ponting and took over at an even more difficult time, when England held sway. However Clarke showed a strong, active style of captaincy being quick to rotate bowlers if the batsmen appeared to be gaining the upper hand and using specific fields to individual batsmen to great effect to restrict favourite scoring shots and to set traps. Darren Lehmann, appointed coach at the beginning of the 2013 tour to England, also undoubtedly made a strong impact. There's little doubt that the pair strengthened Australia in the 2013 series in England but the late appointment of Lehmann limited what could be achieved. The experience of 2013, the additional few months to prepare before 2013/14 and particularly the triumphant return of Mitchell Johnson had a dramatic effect with a 5-0 win in the 2013/14 series. However, the series loss in 2015 showed that a commitment to attacking cricket alone is not enough.

In 2017/18 Steve Smith also showed a strong, active style of captaincy aided by his own supreme individual performances with the bat and clear bowling superiority which resulted in a dominant 4-0 series win. Following the ball-tampering incident in South Africa in March 2018, Smith was removed as captain and cannot be considered again for a management role until March 2020. Tim Paine, who was appointed as Smith's replacement for the remainder of the South African series continued as captain thereafter and captained for the Ashes series in 2019.

As for England an opinion should be given as to who were Australia's greatest captains. Again I'll start with a short list consisting of Monty Noble for his principle, discipline and results during a time of tension between players and authorities, Warwick Armstrong for the dominance of his sides in the period just after the Great War, Bradman for his cricketing brain and leadership through his batting dominance, Richie Benaud for his innovation, willingness to back his judgement and his results at a time when the teams looked broadly even on paper, Allan Border for his commitment to learning and his achievement in turning round the fortunes of the Australian team of the early 1980s and Steve Waugh for his sheer focus on winning and determination to improve a side that was already dominant. Armstrong and Waugh have the top success percentages at 90 and 89 respectively, but as we've acknowledged numbers are not everything here, and the others are in the range of 60 to 71.

As with England I prefer to choose three top captains rather than just one because of the subjectivity involved and the different pressures through the ages. Again, as with England, choosing players whose leadership skills I consider important to their captaincy success, my three top Australian captains would be Monty Noble, Richie Benaud and Steve Waugh with Allan Border close behind. In the same way as for England with Grace and Hutton, there is no doubt that Armstrong and Bradman were very highly effective captains but perhaps they owed more to their stature as a great batsman in Bradman's case and a great all-rounder in Armstrong's and to their great cricket experience.

REVIEW OF RESULTS

In this Chapter I aim to review the results from the average adjustment process for the batsmen, bowlers and all-rounders and to assess whether they give a better quantitative assessment of batsmen and bowlers performances than the raw averages.

I'll also comment more generally on the results for wicketkeepers and captains where the figures are based on a more general approach. Then I can move on in the next chapter to discuss the intrinsic worth of averages in an overall assessment of the merits of players.

I should start with a recap of the broad principle of the adjustment mechanism, what it can compensate for, and just as importantly what it can't compensate for.

As explained earlier, the broad principle is based on the premise that the effect of all the variations in conditions, circumstances and rules over the years has been to change the balance of advantage between batsmen and bowlers and that this results quantitatively in a varying figure for runs per wicket between individual matches and across the ages.

It is to the advantage of a batsman to have played in a match when the average runs per wicket is high, as this is indicative of advantageous conditions for batsmen and a greater chance for any individual batsman to achieve a high score than might otherwise be the case. The same principle applies in reverse for bowlers.

The mechanism as described in chapter 1 therefore seeks to adjust the runs scored for each batsman in each match taking account of the average runs scored per wicket in that match compared to the overall average runs per wicket in Ashes Tests, and thereby to generate an adjusted average. A similar approach is taken for bowlers by adjusting the runs conceded in each match. This can adjust for a multitude of factors that can affect matches including, among others, the fact that early wickets were left uncovered, the weather conditions in any particular match, changes in the LBW and no-ball rules and changes in the quality of cricket bat construction.

It does of course have its limitations. It cannot take account of differing conditions within a match and so a century in the early stages of a game when the pitch may be hard and true is valued in the same way as a century in the later stages when the wicket may have deteriorated. Furthermore, because it only computes one average-runs-per-wicket figure for each match, it treats both sides' batting and bowling in the same way. For example, a century by a player in a team that scores 600 is treated in the same way as a century out of a mere 200 by the side that is batting second and collapses against a magnificent bowling performance by the first side.

Remember also that although the adjustment deals with changes in the overall balance between batsmen and bowlers it treats all categories of bowler in the same way. So at any time in history a particular type of bowling might be more favoured by the prevailing conditions than another. For example, between the second and third eras there was both the change to the LBW rule in 1935, which particularly benefitted off-spinners and the change to the no-ball rule in 1947, which benefitted pace bowlers. These changes created the relative disadvantage for leg spinners, which was briefly discussed in the section on Era 3 bowlers.

One way of attempting to assess the success of the adjustment mechanism is to look at the batsmen and bowlers whose position in the rankings was most affected.

BATSMEN LARGEST RANKINGS MOVEMENT

		ERA	RAW AV	ADJ AV	RAW RK	ADJ RK	MOVT
GRACE	ENG	1	32.29	50.66	53	9	44
TRUMPER	AUS	1	32.79	37.56	52	33	19
HARVEY	AUS	3	38.34	42.89	38	21	17
C HILL	AUS	1	35.46	39.35	42	26	16
MAY	ENG	3	46.05	53.88	19	5	14
HASSETT	AUS	3	38.34	39.24	39	27	12
HENDREN	ENG	2	39.55	31.64	34	56	-22
WOODFULL	AUS	2	44.07	34.03	26	44	-18
COOK	ENG	5	40.21	33.51	33	48	-15
BOON	AUS	4	45.65	37.47	21	34	-13
PONSFORD	AUS	2	47.21	38.70	18	30	-12
HAMMOND	ENG	2	51.85	42.89	10	20	-10
CLARKE	AUS	5	40.75	35.88	31	41	-10

As explained earlier, large movements arise when the average runs per wicket in the matches played by that individual differs substantially from the overall Ashes average of 28.9. The changing conditions over Ashes history have meant that certain eras have higher, and certain eras have lower, run averages than 28.9. Of course, the actual average for each player is entirely specific to him because it depends on the exact matches in which he played. Era 1 and Era 3 contribute most of the large movements upwards and Era 2 contributes many of the large downward movements. Era 5 has produced a number of high-scoring matches as well as average ones, giving some large downward movements which include both Alastair Cook and Michael Clarke. Most of the individual movements have been discussed earlier in the book and the reasons are readily identifiable.

With the bowlers the principles are the same though the movements tend to be greater for the reasons suggested below.

BOWLERS LARGEST RANKINGS MOVEMENT

	🚩	ERA	RAW AV	ADJ AV	RAW RK	ADJ RK	MOVT
TATE	ENG	2	30.60	23.74	37	8	29
MCDERMOTT	AUS	4	26.31	23.04	27	6	21
LAWSON	AUS	4	28.48	24.56	32	14	18
M JOHNSON	AUS	5	25.82	23.89	25	9	16
O'REILLY	AUS	2	25.36	23.24	23	7	16
M HUGHES	AUS	4	30.25	26.25	35	22	13
WARNE	AUS	4/5	23.25	21.15	15	3	12
TURNER	AUS	1	16.53	28.65	2	37	-35
SPOFFORTH	AUS	1	18.41	28.49	5	35	-30
PALMER	AUS	1	21.51	27.10	11	29	-18
LOHMANN	ENG	1	13.01	25.68	1	19	-18
RHODES	ENG	1	24.00	27.88	17	32	-15
BRIGGS	ENG	1	20.55	25.72	6	20	-14
PEEL	ENG	1	16.98	25.14	3	17	-14
GIFFEN	AUS	1	27.09	33.24	29	43	-14

As one would expect, the main movements in rankings for bowlers of particular eras are the reverse of those for batsmen of those eras. The clearest examples are for Era 1 where large adjustments are made to the low raw averages achieved by bowlers who took many wickets in games where the average runs per wicket was very low indeed. In fact, all the large negative movements for bowlers in the table above are for era 1 bowlers. Similarly, the largest positive movement is for Maurice Tate from Era 2, the reverse of the negative movements for many era 2 batsmen, reflecting the high average runs per wicket in many games from that era.

Large adjustments are driven by doing a lot of batting or bowling in matches where the average runs per wicket is either considerably higher or considerably lower than the overall average runs per wicket for Ashes Tests. In both cases it is the better players who are involved.

Good batsmen will stay in longer and obtain higher scores, relative to the average runs per wicket, even in low-scoring games. Bowlers will be asked to continue for many overs before they are taken off. The effect for bowlers tends to be greater because the amount they bowl in each match is at the discretion of the captain, while for batsmen the amount of time they spend at the crease is limited to the time before they get out. Good ones will stay in longer but they don't get a second chance whereas bowlers can bowl more than one bad ball before the skipper takes them off.

BEYOND AVERAGES

I explained in the last chapter why I believe that the adjusted batting and bowling averages set out in this book are a better measure than the commonly used "raw" averages for comparing players in Ashes Test matches and that this is particularly so when the players being compared are from different eras.

However, I have to recognise that any system of averages has its limitations in comparing players. Indeed for many of us, the conclusions that we come to intuitively in evaluating players suggest that it is not a strong average to which we allocate most importance. Rather it is the player's ability to generate match-winning performances and to demonstrate the charisma, influence and motivation to inspire other team members which is most important.

What evidence do I have for making this statement? Let's start by considering Herbert Sutcliffe and Ken Barrington. In the raw averages Sutcliffe and Barrington are the two top ranked English batsmen and in the adjusted averages Sutcliffe remains the top-ranked Englishman with Barrington at fourth. Yet there are few people who would include either of them in their all-time England Ashes team (neither Don Bradman nor Geoff Boycott do so) and CMJ places Sutcliffe only at 43 and Barrington only at 46 in his top 100 cricketers.

Now let's consider Wally Hammond and Denis Compton. They would be in the all-time England Ashes XI for most people (both are chosen by Bradman and Boycott) and are ranked eighth and 21st respectively by CMJ. Yet, Hammond is sixth in the raw average rankings for England and Compton is 12th and they fall to 11th and 14th respectively in the adjusted England listing.[11] So what is it that

---

[11] *Hammond and Compton do fare better in the raw averages of Tests against all teams, but they are both still behind Sutcliffe and Barrington.*

Hammond and Compton had that Sutcliffe and Barrington did not?

There seems to be something about strength of personality and the big occasion. There have only been 14 double centuries scored by English players against Australia and Hammond scored four of them. Next highest is Alastair Cook with two and nobody else has scored more than one. Hammond's aggregate of 905 runs in the series in Australia in 1928/29 is a record for a series in Australia. Not even Bradman has beaten that (his record of 974 runs was in England). Hammond was also a strong captain, useful fast-medium bowler and the top England slip fielder of his time (some would say of all time). In the eight matches in which he scored his nine centuries, England were undefeated, winning six and drawing two despite the fact that Bradman was on the opposing side in six of the eight games.

Compton's record against Australia is not as good as his overall first class and Test records and his standing in the eyes of Bradman and Boycott in selecting their XIs (and certainly in CMJ's eyes when looking at overall performance for his top 100) probably owes something to his non-Ashes performances. It probably also owes a lot to his charisma, and to his batting excellence, which was manifested in a cavalier style. On many occasions he also displayed a courageous fighting spirit against apparently insuperable odds. These qualities tended to inspire not just the England side in the face of overwhelming Australian cricket supremacy, but sometimes seemingly the entire England nation, looking for brightness in a post-war environment darkened by rationing and other day-to-day hardships.

In contrast to Hammond, none of the four Tests in which Compton scored his five centuries was won by England. But in three of the four his was by far the strongest English batting performance. His runs saved two matches that would otherwise have been lost and in the third, when he made his highest Ashes score of 184, he turned what would have been an overwhelming innings defeat into a loss by eight wickets. (The fourth game was a high-scoring draw in which seven centuries, including two double centuries, were scored.)

With the bowlers it is slightly different. Whilst there are great differences in personality, aggression, and charisma between batsmen, there seem to be smaller such differences between bowlers, at least if you look at the separate categories of bowling separately. We expect our pace bowlers to be aggressive characters and generally they are, though clearly there is a difference between Glenn McGrath on the one hand and say Dennis Lillee or Ray Lindwall on the other. We expect the spinners to be more circumspect individuals, though not necessarily all the leg spinners! Overall the bowlers in most preferred all-time Ashes teams, using Bradman's and Boycott's as examples, are likely to be the best performers in the adjusted averages, though not necessarily in the raw averages.

This not only illustrates the point above about personality and charisma being less important as distinguishing factors for bowlers, it is also a recognition of the merit of the overall adjusted average mechanism. The bowlers in the very first years of England v Australia cricket have some very impressive raw averages, but apart from the odd exception they are not considered all-time greats. Most of them are demoted substantially through the adjusted average mechanism, which is both an indication that their low averages have been achieved largely in conditions which are not representative of overall Ashes history, and a validation of some of our intuitive assessments.

Before moving to the next chapter we need to answer that perennial question posed by the title to the book: Was Grace better than Bradman?

To make the comparison, I shall use purely the adjusted average mechanism, which is the primary purpose of this book. Although we have readily acknowledged that averages do not tell the full story I take the view that in leadership and motivational qualities I would not want to distinguish between them. They were very different characters but the extent of the brilliance of both of them meant in my opinion that they were able to motivate their players to an equal extent. However, I have in my application of the adjusted averages tried to compensate for WG not being able to play Test cricket in his prime. My approach has been based on the premise that the only fair way to compare the two players is to look at their performances at comparable ages. For Bradman this means taking just his post-war matches - the 1946/47 and 1948 series - as in all his pre-war matches he was younger than Grace was in any of his matches. In these two series Bradman was aged 38 years and three months to just a few days short of 40 (an average age of just over 39). He played 14 completed innings at an adjusted average of 65.08.

These two series of five matches were played fairly close together and to find a corresponding number of innings for WG one needs to take a slightly longer period. During the period from the beginning of the 1884 series to the end of the 1890 series Grace played 15 completed innings. He was aged 36 (less about a week) at the beginning and 42 years and one month at the end, which is again an average age of about 39 years. In terms of closeness of comparison this seems to be the best fit. Over those 15 completed innings WG had an adjusted average of 53.12.

So, no, Grace was not better than Bradman although the difference between these adjusted averages of 53.12 and 65.08 is nothing like as large as the difference between their respective raw averages of 32.29 and 89.78 for the whole of their Ashes careers.

ALL-TIME TEAMS FOR ENGLAND AND AUSTRALIA

So, which players will be taking the field for the all-time XIs in our, Best of the Best, Ashes Test? In selecting these all-time Ashes teams I have given due regard to the adjusted averages, the concept of which is after all the primary point of this book. However, I have also considered the issues discussed in Chapter 13 to ensure I do not place too much weight on averages, whichever way they are calculated. Twelve players have been selected for each team, so that the actual XI can be chosen on the morning of each game based on the pitch and the weather conditions. It's likely that the optimum balance will be six batsmen, five bowlers and wicket keeper though this may depend on the qualities of any all-rounders selected. The selection is based on performance in England v Australia Tests for which we have the adjusted averages available, rather than performance in all Tests.

Let's take England first.

The England batsmen who feature in the top 20 in the adjusted averages are:

TABLE OVERLEAF

ENGLAND BATSMEN IN TOP 20

		🚩	ERA	ADJ AV	RAW AV	RAW RK
3	SUTCLIFFE	ENG	2	56.42	66.85	2
4	HUTTON	ENG	3	54.21	56.46	7
5	MAY	ENG	3	53.88	46.05	19
7	BARRINGTON	ENG	3	51.07	63.96	4
9	GRACE	ENG	1	50.66	32.29	53
10	HOBBS	ENG	1/2	50.26	54.26	9
12	LEYLAND	ENG	2	49.15	56.83	6
14	BOYCOTT	ENG	3/4	46.28	47.50	17
15	J EDRICH	ENG	3	44.94	48.96	14
18	GOWER	ENG	4	43.88	44.78	24
20	HAMMOND	ENG	2	42.89	51.85	10

All these should certainly be considered and also the next three.

		🚩	ERA	ADJ AV	RAW AV	RAW RK
25	ROOT	ENG	5	39.65	40.33	32
28	PIETERSEN	ENG	5	38.96	44.95	23
31	COMPTON	ENG	3	38.36	42.83	28

Although positioned at tenth overall and sixth in the list of English-men, it would be hard to consider anyone other than Jack Hobbs as the first choice opening batsman for England. For so many years Hobbs was universally acclaimed as England's leading batsman and is still popularly regarded as England's greatest batsman of all time. As explained in Chapter 2, if you look at his pre-First World War performance separately his adjusted average would be more than 60 and second only to Bradman's. This is not to say his performances in the inter-war years were poor—he still had a raw average over 50 and England's dependence on him in the years immediately after the First World War was considerable. He couldn't prevent a 5-0 whitewash in the 1920/21 series but all games lasted at least four days, with two going to five days and one to six. Hobbs totalled 505 runs at 50.5, the next best being Johnny Douglas, the captain, with 354 at 39.3. Hobbs then missed the entire 1921 series (he started the third Test but was taken ill with appendicitis before he had batted). England lost the series 3-0 with two games drawn. Since games in England were restricted to three days and the match at Trent Bridge was lost in two days this was a fairly dismal performance. England used a total of 30 players during the series, the most ever, including no fewer than seven different opening batsmen.

So, let's take Hobbs as the provisional first choice. Provisional only because part of it is based on his universal acclaim and if we find in examining the candidates for his opening partner that there are two who have greater claims than his own, then we should consider going against the consensus of the ages and leave him out. Of the ten Englishmen other than Hobbs in the top 20, five are opening batsmen: Herbert Sutcliffe, Len Hutton, WG Grace, Geoff Boycott and John Edrich.

Sutcliffe was Hobbs's opening partner in 29 Test innings against Australia and they reached 100 on ten occasions. They reached 50 on a further eight occasions and had one unbroken partnership of 32. In these 29 innings Hobbs had an adjusted average of 42.45 and Sutcliffe of 61.42 which gives some idea of Sutcliffe's value to England. Sutcliffe tops the adjusted averages for England with a figure more than six runs per innings ahead of Hobbs himself. Sutcliffe reached 50 in a higher percentage of his innings than any other England player and the success percentage in the games he played was 57.4%, a figure bettered by only five of the featured England players (four of them being bowlers and the other, WG Grace). Sutcliffe was not considered to be the most attractive player to watch, but he accumulated runs outstandingly well. He played the hook and cut with skill but preferred glides through the off side to drives.

Given these statistics why do we not rate him above Hobbs? Much I think derives from the reputation Hobbs acquired before the First World War and the length of his England career which in terms of England v Australia games ran from 1907/08 to 1930.

Before WW1 Hobbs stood out clearly as England's master batsman. He saw the ball early, played with perfect technique, had very quick footwork and would bat according to the conditions usually scoring very quickly. Bradman, who didn't see Hobbs play until 1928 when he was 40 considered him to be without any deficiencies at all and rated him technically the best batsman he ever saw. More than this he provided inspiration to the side and through his perfect charm and manner was a natural ambassador for the game and for his country. Based on his pre-war figures he is ahead of Sutcliffe in the averages. By the time Sutcliffe joined him as his opening partner, Hobbs was the acknowledged No 1 and bore the burden of this leadership position.

Sutcliffe took up that mantle uneasily after Hobbs played his final Test in the 1930 Ashes series. Douglas Jardine, in his book on the 1932/33 Bodyline tour in which he captained England, wrote of Sutcliffe: "Throughout the tour it was clear that he missed his old partner at the other end, and the responsibility of being the senior instead of the junior partner must often have weighed on his mind". This is perhaps reflected in the fact that Sutcliffe's adjusted average for his other 17 Test innings was 47.76 compared with the 61.42 adjusted average for his 29 innings opening with Hobbs.

At the time strike rates were not kept in the way they are now, but it is apparent, from examining the score at the fall of the first wicket in those games in which Hobbs and Sutcliffe opened the batting, that Hobbs usually scored faster in terms of runs per minute. Whether he achieved this by taking more of the strike cannot readily be determined but it must be assumed that this would not always be so. It is a mark of Sutcliffe's respect for Hobbs that he gave his son, who went on to captain Yorkshire in the 1950s, the name Hobbs as one of his middle names. None of this though detracts from the fact that Sutcliffe's own credentials are strong and I will mark him down as provisional opening partner for Hobbs.

During most of Len Hutton's career, which we discussed in Chapter 4, England invariably seemed to be the underdogs. He first played against Australia in the drawn Test series in 1938. The game England won was the final Test at the Oval in which Hutton made his record score of 364. Australia dominated the first three series after the Second World War and Hutton was appointed captain for the 1953 series leading England to victory 1-0 and then retaining the Ashes 3-1 in Australia in 1954/55. As with Hobbs, he had perfect technique and it's notable that a number of his best innings were played in particularly difficult conditions where he alone was able to master them. In 1950/51 at Brisbane he came in at number 8 and scored an unbeaten 62 out of a total innings score of 122, the next highest individual score being 17. At Adelaide in the same series he carried his bat for an undefeated 156 out of a total innings score of 272, the next highest score being 29. At Sydney in 1946/47 he had to retire ill on 122 and England were dismissed for just 280. In 1948 when England collapsed to 52 all out at the Oval, against Ray Lindwall, Keith Miller and Bill Johnston, their lowest total since 1887, Hutton was last out for 30, the next highest score being seven. It seems impossible to leave Hutton out; however there is a case for playing him as well as Sutcliffe thereby leaving the latter to open and preserving the successful opening partnership he built with Hobbs between 1924 and 1930.

Before confirming Hobbs and Sutcliffe, we need to examine the other openers in the top 20: Grace, Boycott and Edrich. Grace's influence on cricket is greater than anyone's and is outlined in Chapter 2. His adjusted average of 50.66 is better than Hobbs's and places him in the top ten of the core players. This was achieved despite the fact that he only played three of his 22 tests before the age of 36 by which time he was past his prime. However, it must be noted, that he played all but three of his games in England, enjoying the home advantage. Rather than disturb the opening partnership of Hobbs and Sutcliffe, I prefer to use WG as an aggressive batsman in the middle order and also possibly as a change bowler. Although he only took nine wickets at 26.8 in Tests against Australia, he took 2,876 wickets in his first class career adopting a slower style during the latter part of his career bowling a moderate leg break with his round arm action.

This leaves Boycott and Edrich. Both were immensely valuable to England in the 1960s and 1970s with Boycott having the stronger reputation for technical correctness and reliability. I have discussed Boycott's career in Chapter 4 above and would particularly note his high success percentage, which emphasises his value to England. I cannot however put either ahead of Hobbs or Sutcliffe and must therefore leave them out.

If Hobbs, Sutcliffe, Hutton and Grace are confirmed, there are two batting places left and the remaining candidates are Peter May, Ken Barrington, Maurice Leyland, David Gower, Wally Hammond, Joe Root, Kevin Pietersen and Denis Compton. Of these players, May has the highest adjusted average at 53.88 and he is ranked fifth among our core players. When Hutton and Compton entered the latter part of their careers in the early to mid-1950s, May took over the role of most consistent and prolific England batsman. He showed his cricketing talent early at Charterhouse School and he recorded a double century against Hampshire by early June 1950, in his first season at Cambridge University.

Exquisite technique and a full range of strokes, especially drives from cover to mid-wicket, were the hallmarks of his play. May made a century on his Test debut against South Africa in 1951 and played two Tests against Australia in 1953 making 39 and 37 batting at No. 3 in the final Test at the Oval, which England won by eight wickets to take the Ashes for the first time in 18 years. On tour to Australia in 1954/55 he recorded his first Ashes century in the second Test at Sydney to help England to a crucial win after an embarrassing loss by an innings at Brisbane, when Hutton had put Australia in to bat. Shy and self-effacing yet confident in his abilities, and with a strong sense of discipline and a tough approach to the game, May was a natural choice to succeed Hutton as captain when Hutton retired in early 1955. After a successful series against South Africa in 1955, May captained England to a successful defence of the Ashes in 1956, topping the series run aggregates with 453 (only one other player managed to reach 300) at a raw average of 90.6. Less successful series against Australia followed in 1958/59, which England lost 4-0, and 1961, which was lost 2-1, but his batting remained strong until the end of the 1961 series when a combination of poor health and increasing business commitments led to his retirement. Ken Barrington's qualities are discussed in Chapters 4 and 13 and although I would like to include him for his effectiveness as a pure accumulator of runs I must rank him behind May. For the final batting place an exciting stroke-playing batsman, who can inspire and win matches, is needed. Barrington's abilities and also those of Leyland are more of the accumulating nature and so I must leave them out. However, four of the batsmen we have yet to discuss: Gower, Hammond, Compton and Pietersen are certainly all exciting stroke-playing batsmen and Joe Root whilst currently perhaps having less of an automatic claim to that description should also be discussed.

Gower was one of England's finest attacking batsmen, possibly the finest left-hander England have had, and is considered by many to have been the most beautiful player to watch of his generation. Peter Roebuck writing about the 1986/87 series in Australia said: "Watching Gower bat is one of life's pleasures, like sipping a gin and tonic as the sun slips over the horizon". Seldom tied down by any bowler, but scoring with text-book shots of all types Gower could be excused some of the indiscretions which occasionally got him out while attempting the over ambitious.

Although Bradman preferred Compton to Gower in his all-time England Ashes team, he regarded Gower as "one of the great natural talents in the history of the game". Furthermore, he rated Gower's innings of 123 at Sydney in 1990/91 as a "masterpiece", "awe-inspiring" and the greatest Ashes innings he saw played in Australia. Gower ranks 18 in the adjusted batting averages, just above Hammond and ties with Hammond for second place in number of centuries against Australia (nine, behind Jack Hobbs's 12). His 732-run aggregate in 1985 is the record for England against Australia in England.

Hammond's position at 20 in the adjusted averages seems low based on his reputation. His attributes are set out in Chapter 13 and his record as a match winner against Australia is outstanding, even if his overall consistency is not so good, this being weakened by his poor performance in his one post-war series. His ability to bowl fast-medium as a change bowler (he took 36 wickets against Australia albeit at a high average, coming on as first change six times and, surprisingly, opening the bowling twice) and his slip-fielding expertise add to his case for inclusion as do his captaincy credentials.

Compton is discussed in both Chapters 4 and 13. He is undoubtedly one of the most charismatic, entertaining and courageous England cricketers. However, his record against Australia is very inconsistent, much more so than Hammond's. Of his three series in Australia only 1946/47 when he amassed 469 runs can be considered a success and 1950/51 with three ducks and no score greater than 23 in seven completed innings was a dismal failure. So, as the selection is based on performance in Ashes Tests he must be left out.

Pietersen's case for inclusion is weakened by the 2013/14 series. He has undoubtedly played brilliant match-winning performances for England, but these have been too few to outweigh his more mediocre innings and so he can't be placed above the other batsmen considered here.

Root has played many solid innings for England but has a poor record of converting 50s to hundreds, not having made an Ashes hundred in his last 11 matches. As a result he has delivered fewer match winning and saving performances for England than he would doubtless expect of himself and given that he also has a poorer adjusted average than both Gower and Hammond he can't currently be considered for this last batting place.

The choice for the final batting place then falls between Gower and Hammond. Gower has a slightly higher adjusted average but Hammond edges ahead because of the sheer dominance of his batting in the late 1920s and early 1930s as evidenced by the record series aggregate for England of 905 and his four double centuries. Furthermore, his bowling and slip fielding also underline his claim. So, the six batsmen selected are: Hobbs, Sutcliffe, Hammond, Hutton, May and Grace.

It is harder to use data to choose our wicketkeeper, than it is for batsmen and bowlers. I have compared wicket keepers in Chapter 10, but no system that I know of can adequately cater for the changes in playing conditions over the years. The data I have given in Chapter 10 makes an addition to the usual data quoted by including the number of wicket-keeping dismissals per ten wickets taken by the team. I consider this to be a more reliable measure than dismissals per match. As explained in Chapter 10 this is simply because a wicket keeper clearly has more opportunity to make dismissals if his side bowl the opposition out twice than he does if the opposition win by an innings and so only bat once. However, there is much more to it than this. If the bowlers knock the stumps over ten times before anybody gets an edge then the wicket keeper hasn't got any chance and it is clear from the overall figures in Chapter 10 that the proportion of wicket keeping dismissals has consistently risen through the ages due no doubt to better equipment, fitness levels, development of swing bowling and so on. Geoff Boycott comments in his book on best Test teams that: "I've always judged keepers not so much by how many catches they take but how many they miss". This must surely be right but data as to keepers' missed catches is not readily available, certainly not for earlier years of Ashes history. So, it's impossible to develop a fully objective method of evaluating keepers' performances as far as I can see.

However, there are some aspects that are easier. There is only one wicket keeper in a side at any time and so there is generally a clear indication who was considered the best in any period. Alan Knott for example played his first game against Australia in 1968 and was never dropped, playing 32 consecutive games against Australia until 1977 when he joined Kerry Packer's WSC. Because he was reaching the end of his career, he was not reinstated in 1979/80 when agreement was reached between Packer and the cricket authorities; however he was recalled for two matches late in 1981. Apart from one match played by Bob Taylor against New Zealand in 1970/71 (to rest Knott and give Taylor some international experience) Knott's run of Test matches against all opposition was similarly unbroken.

Godfrey Evans missed only two matches during his 31-match career against Australia due respectively to sunstroke and a damaged finger. However he was dropped in 1948/9 during the tour of South Africa. Bob Taylor took over from Alan Knott when Knott joined the WSC and played 17 matches against Australia being briefly dropped in favour of Paul Downton at one point as well as in favour of Knott for the last two games of the 1981 series. Alec Stewart, who has the highest position of all the England wicket keepers at No 3 in the ranking shown in Chapter 10 of dismissals per ten wickets, played 33 matches including 26 as wicket keeper between 1990 and 2003. However Russell was preferred as wicketkeeper while Stewart was playing as a batsman for the first three games of 1990/91, Steve Rhodes for two games in 1994/95 and Warren Hegg for two games in 1998/99.

Alan Knott was a superb wicketkeeper for England, setting new standards in fitness and disciplined preparation. He was a fine batsman occasionally batting higher in the order than his normal no 7 or 8. He scored two centuries against Australia and is the only wicket keeper other than Marsh to meet the 1,500-run threshold to be included among the core batsmen. Stewart also qualifies but only by including his runs in the seven matches when he played as specialist batsman and did not keep wicket. Knott has a highly creditable adjusted batting average of 32.20 being ranked 53 overall compared with Stewart's ranking of 58 and adjusted average of 29.84.

His acknowledged position as leading England wicket keeper of his time, his superb keeping and batting record and his status as standard-setter give Knott the position in the side as wicket keeper. Geoff Boycott's comments in his Test teams book, based on his playing career with Knott underline the case for Knott's inclusion.

So, now let's look at our bowlers. Since we have Hammond to use as a fast medium change bowler we can expect to choose three pace bowlers and two slow bowlers in the five places. Before looking at the other bowlers in depth it is worth commenting on Sydney Barnes as he is the most difficult to categorise as a bowler. As a Lancashire League professional for much of his career he was expected to bowl whatever was best for the conditions. He certainly did bowl fast-medium cutters when the conditions warranted it, but he could also bowl both off spin and leg spin. It's quite possible that (rivalled by Sir Gary Sobers) he had the broadest range of bowling skills ever seen in one man and he stands as the fourth ranked English bowler in the adjusted averages behind Jim Laker, Maurice Tate and John Snow. As mentioned in Chapter 1 he was one of two bowlers in the six Giants of the Wisden Century selected by Neville Cardus in 1963.

Barnes has the highest strike rate per match of the England bowlers other than Tom Richardson and would have taken many more wickets but for the off-the-field disputes which kept him out of so many matches. We've discussed his many match-winning performances and he is still regarded by many today as the greatest bowler of them all. It is impossible to leave him out of an all-time England side and although he could bowl at pace and usually opened the bowling for England, I believe he should be regarded primarily as a spinner so that we are left with one spin bowler and three pace bowlers to select.

England have far fewer seam bowlers at the top of the rankings than Australia. Apart from Barnes there are three in the top 20:

ENGLAND PACE BOWLERS
IN TOP 20 BOWLERS

		⚑	ERA	ADJ AV	RAW AV	RAW RK
8	TATE	ENG	2	23.74	30.60	37
13	SNOW	ENG	3	24.40	25.61	24
19	LOHMANN	ENG	1	25.68	13.01	1

Lohmann bowled medium-fast cutters and had a strong record but with Barnes already in the side the need is for specialist spin and pace and so I must leave him out.

Ranked between 20 and 30 are:

		⚑	ERA	ADJ AV	RAW AV	RAW RK
24	TRUEMAN	ENG	3	26.52	25.30	22
25	RICHARDSON	ENG	1	26.64	25.22	21
26	BEDSER	ENG	3	26.82	27.49	30
30	S BROAD	ENG	5	27.16	29.36	33

And we should also acknowledge the other England pace bowlers who have met the qualification condition of 75 wickets. These are:

		⚑	ERA	ADJ AV	RAW AV	RAW RK
34	BOTHAM	ENG	4	28.37	27.65	31
38	WILLIS	ENG	3/4	28.96	26.14	26
40	ANDERSON	ENG	5	30.55	34.57	42

We should only really consider those who meet the qualifying conditions, but I should also mention Harold Larwood and Brian Statham, both of whom are covered in Chapter 8 and are chosen by Geoff Boycott in his squad of 14. Statham had a much better raw average in Tests against other countries than against Australia and though effective on occasions in Ashes Tests has an adjusted average of 32.31, which is too high. Larwood with an overall adjusted average of 24.92 (approximately 20 in the Bodyline series and 30 for the rest) has a case but to put him ahead of John Snow and Fred Trueman one would need to consider the Bodyline tour to be more representative of what he could be expected to achieve than his other ten matches and there really isn't the evidence for this.

Of all the remaining bowlers to consider there is just one, Ian Botham who also meets the batting qualification conditions and can be considered a genuine all-rounder. Moreover, he has taken more wickets against Australia (148) than any other player (Bob Willis has the next highest tally, a full twenty wickets behind Botham at 128). As discussed in Chapter 9 on all-rounders, Botham has delivered many match-winning performances for England, most notably in the 1981 series. He has scored four centuries and taken five wickets in an innings nine times (only Barnes and Richardson have done so more often). He also has the record number of catches for an Englishman other than a wicket keeper at 57. So, it is impossible to leave Botham out.

We now need two further pace bowlers. Maurice Tate, discussed in Chapter 3, was England's most consistently successful pace bowler against Australia in the inter-war years and is the highest ranked England pace bowler by adjusted average. He held England's bowling together in 1924/25, the series in which he took 38 wickets, and he dismissed Bradman five times in the nine matches in which the pair faced each other between 1928/29 and 1930. He is a clear choice.

For the remaining pace bowling place we need someone who is genuinely quick to give the attack hostility comparable with that of the Australians. Of the candidates, Jimmy Anderson and Alec Bedser have much to recommend them but Bedser certainly was not truly quick and at 30.55, Anderson has an adjusted average that is really too high for him to be included. Willis was genuinely quick but is let down by his adjusted average of 28.96. He took five wickets in an innings seven times in his 35 tests a rate of one in five, the same as John Snow with four times out of 20 Tests, but behind Trueman with five from 19 and Stuart Broad with seven from 32.

During his short career, Tom Richardson, achieved the highest strike rate in terms of wickets per match of any bowler in England v Australia Test matches, taking five wickets in an innings no less than

11 times and ten wickets in a match four times in the 14 matches that he played. He and Barnes were the only two bowlers chosen by Neville Cardus in the six top players of the Wisden century in 1963. As mentioned in Chapter 2, Richardson was one of the first true English fast bowlers and the one considered to have inspired the Australians to develop fast bowling. However, the case against him is that he was often expensive and with a success percentage of just 46% his match winning abilities in Ashes tests were not as great as his reputation might suggest.

This leaves John Snow, Stuart Broad and Fred Trueman. Of all England's fast bowlers Trueman is probably the most famous, both for his aggressive approach on the field and his blunt expression both on and off it. He hated batsmen and left them in no doubt of it, but his bluntness of expression came with an astonishingly quick wit, and his amusing repartee made him immensely popular with the average fan. He first played for England in 1952 against India, being released from National Service to play in the four Test matches. He was still on National Service in 1953 when the Australians toured but he was able to obtain release only for the final test in 1953, taking four wickets in the first innings to play his part in regaining the Ashes from Australia. He had several brushes with authority on tour to the West Indies under Hutton's captaincy in 1953/4 and he did not play again while Hutton was captain. He missed both the 1954 series against Pakistan and the tour to Australia in 1954/55 and next played against Australia in 1956 after Hutton had retired and May was captain. In the words of Frank Tyson, "His individuality and non-conformism made him an unstable element in the composition of any tour party".

Trueman went on tour to Australia in 1958/59, playing three matches and taking to six the number of games he played against Australia in the 1950s. He managed to take four or more wickets on just four occasions but only one of these, the last Test in 1953 led to an England victory. His only five-wicket haul in 1956, at Lord's, was overshadowed by Keith Miller's haul of five wickets in both England innings, which guided Australia home by 185 runs in their only win of the series. Trueman then played 13 of the 15 matches in the next three series against Australia in the early 1960s. England won only two of these matches but both victories were in large part as a result of

Trueman's efforts. He took 11 for 88 at Headingley, his home ground, in 1961 to help England to victory by eight wickets, albeit on a pitch that attracted a good deal of criticism. In his last spell in the second innings he took six for five off just less than eight overs bowling off cutters at a reduced pace on May's advice to best exploit the pitch. At Melbourne in 1962/63 he took 8-145 to help England home by seven wickets. It is a pity that Trueman missed so many matches in the 1950s. Just 79 of his 307 test wickets were taken against Australia in the 19 games he played against them.

Trueman of course was not alone among fast bowlers in having a natural belligerence. John Snow was another, although he did not have the outgoing showmanship of Trueman and was more unpredictable. Like Trueman he was genuinely fast and able to swing the ball away from right handers and also bring the ball in off the seam. Coincidentally his first Test against New Zealand in 1965 was Trueman's last. Snow first played against Australia in the 1968 series and in England's tour Down Under in 1970/71 he took 31 wickets. Together with Geoff Boycott's batting Snow's performances were instrumental in the 2-0 series win which saw England regain the Ashes which Australia had held since 1958/59. He then took 24 wickets in the return series in England in 1972 which was drawn 2-2 to ensure the Ashes were retained. By this time he had been involved in two on-field incidents. In Australia in 1970/71 one of his bouncers felled Terry Jenner and in a furious response, the crowd sent a hail of bottles and cans on to the pitch causing England captain Ray Illingworth to temporarily take the side off the field. Against India in 1971 Snow knocked Sunil Gavaskar off his feet as the Indian opener went for a quick run and was subsequently dropped for one Test. He was not selected for the 1974/75 series in Australia where he would have been of great value in redressing the fast bowling balance which then tilted heavily in favour of Australia as Dennis Lillee and Jeff Thomson turned in devastating performances. Snow played his last series against Australia in 1975 before joining Packer's WSC.

Snow took 83 wickets in 20 matches against Australia, a strike rate virtually identical to Trueman's 79 from 19. He took five wickets in an innings four times to Trueman's five. In terms of success percentage Snow is ahead at 52.5% against Trueman's 42%. If the choice between Snow and Trueman were based on performances in all Tests Trueman might well win but based on England v Australia performances, for his better adjusted average and his effectiveness in the 1970/71 and 1972 series, the vote should go to Snow.

Broad recovered from his disappointing series in Australia in 2017/18 to achieve over 20 series wickets again in 2019 as he had in 2013, 2013/04 and 2015. His adjusted average now stands at 27.16 placing him at 30th in the overall adjusted rankings, behind Trueman, Richardson and Bedser but ahead of Botham, Willis and Anderson. In terms of temperament Broad is different from Snow and Trueman. The fast bowler's aggression is just as strong but the belligerence of Snow and Trueman which led to brushes with the authorities is not. Broad has captained England in both T20s and ODIs and although these did not exist in Trueman's day and ODIs only came in to being for the latter part of Snow's it is unlikely that either would have been in the running for the captaincy. Broad's strike rate of wickets per match is behind both Snow and Trueman but his proportion of five wicket hauls is similar and his ability to turn in match-winning performances is just as great, the best examples probably being his 8 for 15 in the first innings of the extraordinary match at Trent Bridge in 2015 and his 11-121 at Durham in 2013. The former is the third best ever bowling analysis in an Ashes innings (behind Laker's 10-53 and 9-37, both at Manchester in 1956).

Broad also now has more Ashes wickets than all England bowlers save Botham and Willis. However, in terms of sheer pace and hostility, essential in my view for this fast bowling slot, I think Broad falls short of both Snow and Trueman. This, together with his higher average means that he misses out and the fast bowling place goes to Snow.

Turning now to the spinners to choose a specialist slow bowler for the last bowling place, Laker at first position overall in the combined adjusted averages is a long way ahead of anyone else with only Bobby Peel in 19th place able to join him in the top 20. In total there are just six England spinners, excluding Barnes who has already been selected, meeting the full qualifying conditions and these are:

TABLE OVERLEAF

ENGLAND SPINNERS

		🚩	ERA	ADJ AV	RAW AV	RAW RK
1	LAKER	ENG	3	19.79	18.27	4
17	PEEL	ENG	1	25.14	16.98	3
20	BRIGGS	ENG	1	25.72	20.55	6
23	UNDERWOOD	ENG	3/4	26.39	26.38	28
32	RHODES	ENG	1	27.88	24.00	17
41	EMBUREY	ENG	4	31.85	34.59	43

Laker's series aggregate of 46 wickets in 1956 is the highest for England v Australia Tests. His figures in the fourth Test at Manchester that year of 19 for 90 remain a record not only for Test cricket but for all first class cricket. Laker was able to take advantage of the favourable 1956 conditions much more than England's left arm spinner Tony Lock and also more than Australia's off spinner Ian Johnson and their leg spinner Richie Benaud. Although Laker's figures are heavily dependent on his five matches in 1956 he did play ten other matches (which brought him 33 wickets at an adjusted average of 29.69) including four in Australia. The adjustment mechanism of course makes allowance for the advantageous conditions for bowlers in 1956 and Laker's fine overall average reflects his greater ability to take advantage of those conditions.

With Laker so far ahead it would take great achievements of a type which could not be valued fully by pure numbers (in the same way as some of the courageous batting performances mentioned above) for anyone to challenge him. All the England spinners mentioned have turned in match-winning performances on occasion but it would be hard to point to instances which are not adequately recognised in the numbers themselves. However, Wilfred Rhodes should be specifically mentioned because of his additional skills with the bat. After all he was one of only four players to meet the qualifying conditions for batting as well as bowling. Do his batting performances sufficiently boost his bowling performances to put him ahead of Laker in overall value to our side? What is our overall assessment of him?

He has a fairly high adjusted average at 27.88, but did deliver some match-winning performances, most notably his 15-wicket haul at Melbourne in 1903/04. As far as his batting is concerned however there were very few matches in which he played significant roles with both bat and ball. In the earlier part of his career he played mainly as a bowler, albeit also being a useful lower order batsman. Conversely, in the latter part of his career when he batted higher up the order (including opening with Hobbs with whom he established a record opening partnership of 323 for England in Tests against Australia) he bowled much less, taking just nine wickets in 14 matches between 1911 and 1921. This is not enough to displace Laker.

Although only bowlers meeting the qualifying conditions should strictly be considered, I can't ignore the fact that Bradman chose Hedley Verity (mentioned in Chapter 8) ahead of Jim Laker for the spin bowling slot in his all-time England team. The Don faced both bowlers, although Laker only once in the 1948 series when the Englishman did not perform well. Other than his match-winning 15 for 104 at Lord's in 1934, Verity's best was eight wickets in the final Test of the Bodyline series at Sydney when England had already won the Ashes. It is true that he had a great capacity to bowl tightly on good wickets but given the limited spin bowling that can be included in the England twelve, a good strike rate of wickets per match is a further relevant numerical factor and one that is not measured in the adjusted averages. Verity' strike rate of 3.3 wickets per match including the 15 wickets at Lord's is too low to displace Laker, (who had a strike rate of 5.3) and Laker's choice for the final bowling place is therefore confirmed

So, that gives us our all-time top Ashes team.

TABLE OVERLEAF

ALL-TIME TOP ASHES TEAM - ENGLAND

1. **JACK HOBBS**
2. **HERBERT SUTCLIFFE**
3. **LEN HUTTON**
4. **WALTER HAMMOND**
5. **PETER MAY**
6. **WG GRACE (CPT)**
7. **IAN BOTHAM**
8. **ALAN KNOTT (WKT)**
9. **MAURICE TATE**
10. **JOHN SNOW**
11. **JIM LAKER**
12. **SYDNEY BARNES**

But who should lead them to face the Australians? Of the players who made our team, Hammond, May, Hutton, Grace and Botham have captained England. As described in Chapter 11, Botham was not a successful captain and May, though successful in 1956 was much less so afterwards. Hammond, who began as a professional and became an amateur in order to have the opportunity to captain England, was introspective and not proactively encouraging, especially of his younger teammates, though he set an impeccable example. This leaves Hutton and Grace on the shortlist in Chapter 11 for the top England captains. Hutton, successful though he was, was a cautious captain and prone to over worry. The choice has to be WG Grace who alone had the supreme self confidence to captain England with assurance and also to bat, bowl and field with undiminished effectiveness. Grace also at 69% had the highest success percentage as a captain of the five candidates here, although Hutton at 65% ran him close.

***

Now let's turn to Australia. As with England let's start with the assumption that we will choose six batsmen, five bowlers and one wicketkeeper, although this may vary slightly if we choose an all-rounder.

Bradman will clearly play at No. 3, but who will be the opening batsmen?

AUSTRALIANS AFTER BRADMAN IN TOP 20 BATSMEN

The eight Australians after Bradman in the batting top 20 are:

			ERA	ADJ AV	RAW AV	RAW RK
2	S SMITH	AUS	5	57.52	65.12	3
6	S WAUGH	AUS	4	53.75	58.18	5
8	BORDER	AUS	4	51.01	56.31	8
11	M WAUGH	AUS	4	49.27	50.09	13
13	MORRIS	AUS	3	48.02	50.73	11
16	G CHAPPELL	AUS	3/4	44.91	45.94	20
17	LANGER	AUS	5	44.46	50.24	12
19	SLATER	AUS	4	42.94	45.10	22

This includes three opening batsmen in Arthur Morris, Justin Langer and Michael Slater. Outside the top 20 are:

			ERA	ADJ AV	RAW AV	RAW RK
22	LAWRY	AUS	3	41.43	48.54	15
29	M TAYLOR	AUS	4	38.76	42.30	29
30	PONSFORD	AUS	2	38.70	47.21	18
33	TRUMPER	AUS	1	37.56	32.79	52
37	D WARNER	AUS	5	37.10	39.39	35
39	REDPATH	AUS	3	36.09	38.76	36
44	WOODFULL	AUS	2	34.03	44.07	26

This is a difficult selection and I'll start with the views of Bradman, Boycott and CMJ. (David Warner, of course, who played his first Test match in 2011 was not known to Bradman or CMJ and came after Boycott's book was published in 2008). Bradman chooses Morris and Bill Ponsford, both of whom he played with extensively during his career. Boycott chooses Morris and Victor Trumper. CMJ rates only Trumper at 30 and Ponsford at 81 in his top 100 leaving out all the other openers mentioned here including Morris. Langer played between 1998 and 2007 and so would not have been considered by Bradman, who confirmed his selection in 2000, but would have been well known to Boycott, whose book was published in 2008 and to CMJ whose book was published in 2009. Mark Taylor played his last Ashes Test in 1999 and would have been well known to all three, as would Slater who played his last Ashes Test in 2001. With the exception of Trumper none of the Australian openers have the same motivational qualities found in Hobbs, Hutton and Grace and so the process of choosing the Australian openers is more analytical than it was for the England team.

Consistency is most important in opening batsmen and the following table shows the proportion of times that the openers mentioned have passed 30, a score which might be expected, together with a comparable performance from the other opener, to achieve an opening partnership of 50:

AUSTRALIAN OPENERS

(in order of highest % of 30s)

	ERA	INNS	NOs < 30	30s	%
WOODFULL	2	41	1	20	50.0
LAWRY	3	51	2	24	49.0
REDPATH	3	43	3	19	47.5
LANGER	5	38	2	17	47.2
M TAYLOR	4	61	0	28	44.3
D WARNER	5	43	0	19	44.2
MORRIS	3	43	0	19	44.2
PONSFORD	2	35	1	15	44.1
SLATER	4	37	0	16	43.2
TRUMPER	1	74	3	24	33.8

Bill Woodfull comes out top here, followed by Bill Lawry. However, with the exception of Trumper the percentage of 30s does not vary over-much and with Morris leading by adjusted average and given his selection by both Boycott and Bradman, his position of No 1 opening batsman should be confirmed.

Since Morris is a left-hander and a right/left opening partnership might be preferred, this would favour Slater, Ponsford, Trumper, Bill Woodfull and Ian Redpath over Langer, Lawry and Taylor. Of the right handers though, only Woodfull and Redpath score highly for consistency in the table below and their adjusted averages are the two lowest of the batsmen featured here. Of the left handers Langer is ahead of Taylor on both adjusted average and on consistency as measured in the table above. Lawry's consistency is not greatly higher than that of Langer and Lawry's claim is negated to some extent by his reputation for ultra-defensiveness. A point in favour of Lawry is that virtually throughout his career he was playing against Trueman or Snow, two of England's foremost fast bowlers in Ashes history. However, I consider that Australian sides perform best when playing positive aggressive cricket and this suggests Lawry should be excluded. On this basis Langer is chosen as Morris's partner.

With Bradman at number 3, this leaves us with three batting slots to choose. The consensus through the ages as to the virtues of Trumper cannot be disregarded and we must accept that on his day he must have had no equal. However the figures show him to have been somewhat inconsistent and as much as one might like to include him as a middle-order, stroke-playing batsman, this cannot really be justified when there are other fast-scoring batsmen with much higher averages, namely Steve Smith, the Waugh brothers, Allan Border, and Greg Chappell who are all in the top 20 with averages above 40. Of these, Steve Smith, now second only to Bradman in the overall ranking has a clear lead by way of adjusted average following his outstanding performances in the 2017/18 and 2019 series and cannot be left out.

There are now two batting places left to fill and four batsmen in the top 20, Steve Waugh, Allan Border, Mark Waugh, and Greg Chappell. From the batsmen just outside the top 20, both Neil Harvey and Charlie Macartney were in Bradman's Ashes team and deserve a mention. Bradman approved of Harvey's positive approach to batting, his fielding and also liked to have him as an additional left hander to Morris in the side. However, his adjusted average at 42.89 is well below Border, also a left hander, and the Waugh brothers. Macartney's adjusted average is a little lower still than Harvey's, at just over 40 but he was an explosive batsman and also a useful left-arm slow bowler who took 33 Ashes wickets at 32.29 apiece. However, as most of his wickets were taken before World War One when, as we have discussed, pitches were of an inconsistent standard, the case for his bowling to be given real weight is weakened. The balance of batting and other skills we need for these two places may be affected by the choice of bowlers and wicket keeper and so it may be best to move to these first and then revisit the last two batting places.

No fewer than ten of the top 20 places in the bowling adjusted averages are filled by Australian pace bowlers as follows:

AUSTRALIAN PACE BOWLERS IN TOP 20 BOWLERS

		🏴	ERA	ADJ AV	RAW AV	RAW RK
2	MCGRATH	AUS	4/5	20.39	20.92	8
4	ALDERMAN	AUS	4	22.15	21.17	10
5	LILLEE	AUS	3/4	22.41	21.00	9
6	MCDERMOTT	AUS	4	23.04	26.31	27
9	M JOHNSON	AUS	5	23.89	25.82	25
10	LINDWALL	AUS	3	24.02	22.44	14
11	THOMSON	AUS	3/4	24.09	24.18	18
12	MILLER	AUS	3	24.20	22.40	13
14	LAWSON	AUS	4	24.56	28.48	32
16	DAVIDSON	AUS	3	24.97	23.76	16

Outside the top 20 are:

		🏴	ERA	ADJ AV	RAW AV	RAW RK
21	JOHNSTON	AUS	3	25.94	24.24	19
22	M HUGHES	AUS	4	26.25	30.25	35
27	SIDDLE	AUS	5	26.84	29.81	34
35	SPOFFORTH	AUS	1	28.49	18.41	5
36	MCKENZIE	AUS	3	28.57	31.34	38

Glenn McGrath is not only first of the Australian bowlers by adjusted average but is third in the list of wicket takers behind Shane Warne and Dennis Lillee. In each of six consecutive series from 1997 to 2006/07 he took 19 wickets or more. His prominence is universally acknowledged, as discussed in Chapter 5, and he is clearly required for the team. As McGrath was of fast-medium pace, specialising in movement off the seam, the pace attack would be nicely balanced with two genuinely quick bowlers.

Next in the adjusted averages is Terry Alderman. Like McGrath, Alderman was not genuinely quick and his reliance on swing was more suited to English conditions, his 17 wickets in Australia costing a raw average of just over 30. Apart from Alan Davidson all the others listed above are genuinely quick.

Craig McDermott was not as fiery as Lillee, Jeff Thomson, Ray Lindwall, Keith Miller or Mitchell Johnson and his career was affected by injuries. After playing in the 1985 series in England he only played four games in the next four series (in one of these at Perth in 1990/91 he took his only ten-wicket haul). He then played in one more series in 1994/95. As well as being fifth in the adjusted averages, Lillee's tally of 167 Ashes wickets is second only to Warne's 195, and he is fourth in wickets-per-match behind Tom Richardson, Charlie Turner and Terry Alderman.

Mitchell Johnson, at ninth in the rankings, took 37 wickets in the 2013/14 series, the record for an Australian in a five-match Test series in Australia against England. With a raw average of just 13.97, he was the driving force behind the hosts' 5-0 series victory. Bowling at over 90 mph with a slinging action, he achieved a level of hostility not seen since Lillee and Thomson some 30 years previously. He has however been prone to inconsistency, occasionally finding it difficult to control his direction and he loses out to Lillee because of Lillee's greater strike rate and consistency.

Like Lillee, Lindwall was a hostile fast bowler but the pair had different characteristics. Lillee had a fiery temperament, similar to Fred Trueman. His approach to the wicket exuded explosive energy and culminated in a giant leap, his left foot banging into the ground and extracting maximum bounce from the pitch. In contrast, Lindwall was rhythmically smooth and his bouncer would skid through at throat or high-chest level. Lillee's aggression spilled over into incidents with opposing players whereas Lindwall was more controlled. However, Lillee wins the vote to join McGrath in the team due not only to his slightly superior average but also his superior strike rate. Both he and Lindwall played in 29 Ashes Tests with Lillee taking 167 wickets, compared to Lindwall's 114.

Thomson certainly was lethal in the 1974/75 series when he took 33 wickets at 17.93 raw average from five of the six tests (Lillee took 25 at 23.84 from all six tests). However both Thomson and Lawson are behind Lillee on number of wickets, average, consistency and strike rate. It's possible that Thomson's hostility and superior strike rate could place him ahead of Lindwall but it's unclear whether we would wish to select either of them given that McGrath and Lillee are already selected.

Miller had a lower wicket tally and strike rate than those mentioned above and that can be at least partly attributed to a back injury which occasionally prevented him from bowling and the fact that he regularly played alongside Lindwall and Bill Johnston, who would often open the bowling. As mentioned in Chapter 3, Miller was not as consistently fast as Lindwall but his fastest deliveries were just as quick. He is also the only Australian bowler who can be considered for the all-time team and who also meets the batting qualification conditions. With a batting adjusted average of 33.67 and ranking of 46 he is above four England opening batsmen. And for that reason, along with his ranking by adjusted average, he has the strongest claim for the third pace bowling slot, albeit as an all-rounder.

AUSTRALIAN SPINNERS

The Australian spin bowlers in the core adjusted averages are:

		⚑	ERA	ADJ AV	RAW AV	RAW RK
3	WARNE	AUS	4/5	21.15	23.25	15
7	O'REILLY	AUS	2	23.24	25.36	23
18	TRUMBLE	AUS	1	25.59	20.88	7
28	GRIMMETT	AUS	2	26.99	32.44	40
29	PALMER	AUS	1	27.10	21.51	11
31	MAILEY	AUS	2	27.39	34.12	41
33	NOBLE	AUS	1	28.33	24.86	20
37	TURNER	AUS	1	28.65	16.53	2
39	LYON	AUS	5	29.60	30.53	36
42	BENAUD	AUS	3	32.98	31.81	39
43	GIFFEN	AUS	1	33.24	27.09	29

Charlie Turner was a medium to medium-fast paced bowler who bowled fast off breaks, and he is listed here because he could not be in serious contention for the pace bowling slots. Shane Warne and Bill O'Reilly are a long way ahead of the others in all measures except possibly strike rate where Turner is high. But Turner and Joey Palmer have high averages and can't merit serious comparison with Warne and O'Reilly.

As discussed in Chapter 5, although Bradman preferred Clarrie Grimmett to Warne in his Ashes teams I consider based on Ashes Tests and adjusted averages that Warne has much the stronger case. However the standing of any opinion given by Bradman means that more needs to be said to be sure that the choice of Warne is the right one.

Certainly the case for Warne is supported both by Geoff Boycott's choice of Warne over Grimmett and by CMJ's ranking of Warne as 4th overall in cricketing history, the highest ranked England/Australian cricketer since Bradman. If further evidence were needed, one should perhaps look at ten-wicket match and five-wicket innings hauls as a measure of match-winning ability. Warne has four ten-wicket hauls from his 36 matches compared with two ten wicket hauls from 22 matches for Grimmett. This is fairly even. Both men have eleven five-wicket hauls, although Grimmett played significantly fewer games. I suggest though that this is misleading as in Grimmett's era a much greater proportion of the bowling was done by spinners, as evidenced by the fact that three of the four bowlers meeting the bowling qualification condition in Grimmett's era were spin bowlers. In Warne's era pace bowlers were the leading wicket takers, indeed the only spin bowlers other than Warne from the fourth and fifth eras (1977 onwards) who meet the qualifying conditions are Nathan Lyon and John Emburey. If one looks at four-wicket innings hauls, something which might be more feasible for Warne when the pace bowlers are dominating then he has 26 from his 36 games to Grimmett's 13 from 22 games. Warne nevertheless has managed to achieve a strike rate per match of 5.4 compared with Grimmett's 4.8, in addition to an adjusted average which is nearly six runs per wicket better than Grimmett's.

Warne, O'Reilly, Grimmett and Arthur Mailey were all leg-spin bowlers. Hugh Trumble was an off spinner, as is Nathan Lyon, and Monty Noble bowled off-breaks at a faster, broadly medium, pace.

Noble is the only one of the slower bowlers who also meets the batting conditions and has an adjusted average of 33.54, just one place below Miller in the batting rankings. However, given O'Reilly bowled his leg spin at a faster pace, there is sufficient variety between him and Warne not to need a third slow bowler.

This takes us to the choice of wicket keeper. Chapter 9 discusses the difficulties in comparing wicketkeepers across the ages and nine of the 15 wicket keepers meeting the qualification of 50 dismissals are Australian. In order of dismissals per ten wickets they are as follows (the table includes the span of their careers as well as their adjusted batting average).

AUSTRALIAN WICKETKEEPERS

		D/10 W	ADJ AV	SPAN
1	GILCHRIST	2.55	42.41	2001-07
2	HADDIN	2.38	36.97	2009-15
4	HEALY	2.25	29.54	1989-99
5	GROUT	2.18	13.67	1958-66
7	R MARSH	2.03	28.33	1970-83
12	OLDFIELD	1.54	20.21	1920-37
13	CARTER	1.48	27.10	1907-21
14	BLACKHAM	1.14	24.02	1877-94
15	KELLY	1.03	20.61	1896-1905

Adam Gilchrist and Brad Haddin, the most recent keepers, top this list both for dismissals per ten wickets and for adjusted batting average. The batting averages are comparable across the ages because of the adjustment mechanism but the dismissals per ten wickets are not. The evidence shows that wicket keeping dismissals have increased through the ages and so the earlier keepers' figures must be seen in this context.

In particular, Wally Grout must be considered a rival to some of the later keepers. However his batting average is poor and Gilchrist leads the keepers' rankings not only in terms of dismissals per ten wickets, but also in terms of batting with an adjusted average that would put him at position 22 in the batting rankings if he had made the qualifying 1,500 runs rather than his actual 1,083. More than that, he scored at a strike rate of 92 runs per 100 balls equivalent to 5.5 runs per over, more than twice the rate of the slow scoring 1950s and early 1960s. Despite Haddin having an excellent series in 2013/14, when he achieved a run aggregate of 493 in which he reached 50 in six of the eight innings he played, Gilchrist has to be the choice as keeper.

This means that we have Morris, Langer, Bradman and Steve Smith chosen as four batsmen, Gilchrist as keeper, Lillee, McGrath and Miller as pace bowlers and Warne and O'Reilly as spin bowlers. Two more batsmen are needed. With Gilchrist there as a fast-scoring left hander and two left-handed openers, Harvey now loses out on the basis of adjusted average as does Macartney. This leaves Steve Waugh, Allan Border, Mark Waugh, and Greg Chappell who are compared in the following table:

AUSTRALIAN BATSMEN FOR MIDDLE ORDER PLACES

	ADJ AV	STRIKE RATE	CATCHES PER MTCH	WKTS	BOWLING RAW AVGE	WKTS PER MTCH
S WAUGH	53.75	54	0.6	22	41.5	0.5
BORDER	51.01	43	1.2	4	93.5	0.1
M WAUGH	49.27	56	1.5	14	37.1	0.5
G CHAPPELL	44.91	46	1.7	13	52.2	0.4

Steve Waugh, with the highest adjusted average and strike rate, scores most strongly and, in comparison with Border, Mark Waugh's superior strike rate and bowling support are enough to take the second place notwithstanding Border's higher average. Chappell's lower average and strike rate place him behind the other three. If performance in all Test matches were considered, the choice for the final batting place could be different as Greg Chappell has the highest all-Test raw average of all four players here and is a full 12 runs ahead of Mark Waugh. But using our criterion of adjusted averages in Ashes Tests it is Mark Waugh who is ahead by over four runs and he can be considered as Greg Chappell's equal as a talented stroke player.

This makes the twelve:

ALL-TIME TOP ASHES TEAM - AUSTRALIA

1. **ARTHUR MORRIS**
2. **JUSTIN LANGER**
3. **DON BRADMAN**
4. **STEVE SMITH**
5. **MARK WAUGH**
6. **STEVE WAUGH (CPT)**
7. **ADAM GILCHRIST (WKT)**
8. **KEITH MILLER**
9. **SHANE WARNE**
10. **DENNIS LILLEE**
11. **BILL O'REILLY**
12. **GLENN MCGRATH**

Who should captain the side? This is a question worthy of much debate which could generate strong opinions. Notwithstanding the conclusions in Chapter 10, which place Steve Waugh ahead of Bradman on captaincy skills, it may well have been the case that if all had played in the same side, Bradman would have been captain due to the traditional Australian practice of selecting the strongest batsman to lead the team. More modern practice, though favouring batsmen, would prize other skills including ability to work with the off-field coach. It can't be known how Bradman would have fared with that. I have though to remain true to the conclusion reached in Chapter 10 and to appoint Steve Waugh. He also reflects the balance of the side which includes more players from later eras than from those in which Bradman played.

What is most striking about the respective England and Australia sides is the different spread of players from different eras between them. For England seven of the 12 players played at least some of their Ashes Tests before World War Two and none played any Ashes Tests after 1989. For Australia only two played any Ashes Tests before World War Two, while seven played after 1989 including of course Steve Smith who has displaced Allan Border from the Australian team chosen in the first edition of the book published in December 2017.

APPENDIX

BATSMEN IN ORDER OF RUNS SCORED

		🏳	ERA	M	R	RAW AV	RAW RK	ADJ AV	ADJ RK
1	BRADMAN	AUS	2	37	5028	89.78	1	73.73	1
2	HOBBS	ENG	1/2	41	3636	54.26	9	50.26	10
3	BORDER	AUS	4	47	3548	56.31	8	51.01	8
4	GOWER	ENG	4	42	3269	44.78	24	43.88	18
5	S WAUGH	AUS	4	46	3200	58.18	5	53.75	6
6	BOYCOTT	ENG	3/4	38	2945	47.50	17	46.28	14
7	HAMMOND	ENG	2	33	2852	51.85	10	42.89	20
8	S SMITH	AUS	5	27	2800	65.12	3	57.52	2
9	SUTCLIFFE	ENG	2	27	2741	66.85	2	56.42	3
10	C HILL	AUS	1	41	2660	35.46	42	39.35	26
11	J EDRICH	ENG	3	32	2644	48.96	14	44.94	15
12	GOOCH	ENG	4	42	2632	33.31	49	31.07	57
13	G CHAPPELL	AUS	3/4	35	2619	45.94	20	44.91	16
14	M TAYLOR	AUS	4	33	2496	42.30	29	38.76	29
15	COOK	ENG	5	35	2493	40.21	33	33.51	48
16	PONTING	AUS	5	35	2476	44.21	25	38.01	32
17	COWDREY	ENG	3	43	2433	34.26	46	35.05	43
18	HUTTON	ENG	3	27	2428	56.46	7	54.21	4
19	HARVEY	AUS	3	37	2416	38.34	38	42.89	21
20	TRUMPER	AUS	1	40	2263	32.79	52	37.56	33
21	CLARKE	AUS	5	35	2241	40.75	31	35.88	41
22	BOON	AUS	4	31	2237	45.65	21	37.47	34
23	LAWRY	AUS	3	29	2233	48.54	15	41.43	22
24	M WAUGH	AUS	4	29	2204	50.09	13	49.27	11
25	S GREGORY	AUS	1	52	2193	25.80	61	27.48	61
26	ARMSTRONG	AUS	1	42	2172	35.03	45	37.11	36
27	PIETERSEN	ENG	5	27	2158	44.95	23	38.96	28
28	I CHAPPELL	AUS	3	30	2138	41.11	30	37.26	35
29	BARRINGTON	ENG	3	23	2111	63.96	4	51.07	7
30	MORRIS	AUS	3	24	2080	50.73	11	48.02	13
31	BELL	ENG	5	33	1983	35.41	43	32.85	52

			ERA	M	R	RAW AV	RAW RK	ADJ AV	ADJ RK
32	WALTERS	AUS	3	36	1981	35.38	44	33.02	50
33	MCCABE	AUS	2	24	1931	48.27	16	39.84	24
34	MACLAREN	ENG	1	35	1931	33.87	47	35.98	40
35	NOBLE	AUS	1	39	1905	30.72	56	33.52	47
36	ATHERTON	ENG	4	33	1900	29.68	58	27.62	60
37	COMPTON	ENG	3	28	1842	42.83	28	38.36	31
38	A STEWART	ENG	4	33	1810	30.67	57	29.84	58
39	HAYWARD	ENG	1	29	1747	35.65	41	36.30	38
40	HENDREN	ENG	2	28	1740	39.55	34	31.64	56
41	RHODES	ENG	1	41	1706	31.01	54	33.51	49
42	LEYLAND	ENG	2	20	1705	56.83	6	49.15	12
43	ROOT	ENG	5	24	1694	40.33	32	39.65	25
44	KNOTT	ENG	3/4	34	1682	32.98	51	32.20	53
45	WOODFULL	AUS	2	25	1675	44.07	26	34.03	44
46	BOTHAM	ENG	4	36	1673	29.35	59	32.00	55
47	SLATER	AUS	4	20	1669	45.10	22	42.94	19
48	WOOLLEY	ENG	2	32	1664	33.28	50	32.13	54
49	GATTING	ENG	4	27	1661	37.75	40	34.01	45
50	LANGER	AUS	5	21	1658	50.24	12	44.46	17
51	MACARTNEY	AUS	1/2	26	1640	43.15	27	40.19	23
52	R MARSH	AUS	3/4	42	1633	27.21	60	28.33	59
53	J DARLING	AUS	1	31	1632	30.79	55	32.99	51
54	D WARNER	AUS	5	23	1615	39.39	35	37.10	37
55	HUSSAIN	ENG	4/5	23	1581	38.56	37	35.12	42
56	HASSETT	AUS	3	24	1572	38.34	39	39.24	27
57	MAY	ENG	3	21	1566	46.05	19	53.88	5
58	PONSFORD	AUS	2	20	1558	47.21	18	38.70	30
59	REDPATH	AUS	3	23	1512	38.76	36	36.09	39
60	MILLER	AUS	3	29	1511	33.57	48	33.67	46
61	GRACE	ENG	1	22	1098	32.29	53	50.66	9

BATSMEN RAW RANKINGS

		⚑	ERA	RAW AV	ADJ AV	ADJ RK
1	BRADMAN	AUS	2	89.78	73.73	1
2	SUTCLIFFE	ENG	2	66.85	56.42	3
3	S SMITH	AUS	5	65.12	57.52	2
4	BARRINGTON	ENG	3	63.96	51.07	7
5	S WAUGH	AUS	4	58.18	53.75	6
6	LEYLAND	ENG	2	56.83	49.15	12
7	HUTTON	ENG	3	56.46	54.21	4
8	BORDER	AUS	4	56.31	51.01	8
9	HOBBS	ENG	1/2	54.26	50.26	10
10	HAMMOND	ENG	2	51.85	42.89	20
11	MORRIS	AUS	3	50.73	48.02	13
12	LANGER	AUS	5	50.24	44.46	17
13	M WAUGH	AUS	4	50.09	49.27	11
14	J EDRICH	ENG	3	48.96	44.94	15
15	LAWRY	AUS	3	48.54	41.43	22
16	MCCABE	AUS	2	48.27	39.84	24
17	BOYCOTT	ENG	3/4	47.50	46.28	14
18	PONSFORD	AUS	2	47.21	38.70	30
19	MAY	ENG	3	46.05	53.88	5
20	G CHAPPELL	AUS	3/4	45.94	44.91	16
21	BOON	AUS	4	45.65	37.47	34
22	SLATER	AUS	4	45.10	42.94	19
23	PIETERSEN	ENG	5	44.95	38.96	28
24	GOWER	ENG	4	44.78	43.88	18
25	PONTING	AUS	5	44.21	38.01	32
26	WOODFULL	AUS	2	44.07	34.03	44
27	MACARTNEY	AUS	1/2	43.15	40.19	23
28	COMPTON	ENG	3	42.83	38.36	31
29	M TAYLOR	AUS	4	42.30	38.76	29
30	I CHAPPELL	AUS	3	41.11	37.26	35

			ERA	RAW AV	ADJ AV	ADJ RK
31	CLARKE	AUS	5	40.75	35.88	41
32	ROOT	ENG	5	40.33	39.65	25
33	COOK	ENG	5	40.21	33.51	48
34	HENDREN	ENG	2	39.55	31.64	56
35	D WARNER	AUS	5	39.39	37.10	37
35	REDPATH	AUS	3	38.76	36.09	39
37	HUSSAIN	ENG	4/5	38.56	35.12	42
38	HARVEY	AUS	3	38.34	42.89	21
39	HASSETT	AUS	3	38.34	39.24	27
40	GATTING	ENG	4	37.75	34.01	45
41	HAYWARD	ENG	1	35.65	36.30	38
42	C HILL	AUS	1	35.46	39.35	26
43	BELL	ENG	5	35.41	32.85	52
44	WALTERS	AUS	3	35.38	33.02	50
45	ARMSTRONG	AUS	1	35.03	37.11	36
46	COWDREY	ENG	3	34.26	35.05	43
47	MACLAREN	ENG	1	33.87	35.98	40
48	MILLER	AUS	3	33.57	33.67	46
49	GOOCH	ENG	4	33.31	31.07	57
50	WOOLLEY	ENG	2	33.28	32.13	54
51	KNOTT	ENG	3/4	32.98	32.20	53
52	TRUMPER	AUS	1	32.79	37.56	33
53	GRACE	ENG	1	32.29	50.66	9
54	RHODES	ENG	1	31.01	33.51	49
55	J DARLING	AUS	1	30.79	32.99	51
56	NOBLE	AUS	1	30.72	33.52	47
57	A STEWART	ENG	4	30.67	29.84	58
58	ATHERTON	ENG	4	29.68	27.62	60
59	BOTHAM	ENG	4	29.35	32.00	55
60	R MARSH	AUS	3/4	27.21	28.33	59
61	S GREGORY	AUS	1	25.80	27.48	61

BATSMEN ADJUSTED RANKINGS

		⚑	ERA	ADJ AV	RAW AV	RAW RK
1	BRADMAN	AUS	2	73.73	89.78	1
2	S SMITH	AUS	5	57.52	65.12	3
3	SUTCLIFFE	ENG	2	56.42	66.85	2
4	HUTTON	ENG	3	54.21	56.46	7
5	MAY	ENG	3	53.88	46.05	19
6	S WAUGH	AUS	4	53.75	58.18	5
7	BARRINGTON	ENG	3	51.07	63.96	4
8	BORDER	AUS	4	51.01	56.31	8
9	GRACE	ENG	1	50.66	32.29	53
10	HOBBS	ENG	1/2	50.26	54.26	9
11	M WAUGH	AUS	4	49.27	50.09	13
12	LEYLAND	ENG	2	49.15	56.83	6
13	MORRIS	AUS	3	48.02	50.73	11
14	BOYCOTT	ENG	3/4	46.28	47.50	17
15	J EDRICH	ENG	3	44.94	48.96	14
16	G CHAPPELL	AUS	3/4	44.91	45.94	20
17	LANGER	AUS	5	44.46	50.24	12
18	GOWER	ENG	4	43.88	44.78	24
19	SLATER	AUS	4	42.94	45.10	22
20	HAMMOND	ENG	2	42.89	51.85	10
21	HARVEY	AUS	3	42.89	38.34	38
22	LAWRY	AUS	3	41.43	48.54	15
23	MACARTNEY	AUS	1/2	40.19	43.15	27
24	MCCABE	AUS	2	39.84	48.27	16
25	ROOT	ENG	5	39.65	40.33	32
26	C HILL	AUS	1	39.35	35.46	42
27	HASSETT	AUS	3	39.24	38.34	39
28	PIETERSEN	ENG	5	38.96	44.95	23
29	M TAYLOR	AUS	4	38.76	42.30	29
30	PONSFORD	AUS	2	38.70	47.21	18

			ERA	ADJ AV	RAW AV	RAW RK
31	COMPTON	ENG	3	38.36	42.83	28
32	PONTING	AUS	5	38.01	44.21	25
33	TRUMPER	AUS	1	37.56	32.79	52
34	BOON	AUS	4	37.47	45.65	21
35	I CHAPPELL	AUS	3	37.26	41.11	30
36	ARMSTRONG	AUS	1	37.11	35.03	45
37	D WARNER	AUS	5	37.10	39.39	35
38	HAYWARD	ENG	1	36.30	35.65	41
39	REDPATH	AUS	3	36.09	38.76	36
40	MACLAREN	ENG	1	35.98	33.87	47
41	CLARKE	AUS	5	35.88	40.75	31
42	HUSSAIN	ENG	4/5	35.12	38.56	37
43	COWDREY	ENG	3	35.05	34.26	46
44	WOODFULL	AUS	2	34.03	44.07	26
45	GATTING	ENG	4	34.01	37.75	40
46	MILLER	AUS	3	33.67	33.57	48
47	NOBLE	AUS	1	33.52	30.72	56
48	COOK	ENG	5	33.51	40.21	33
49	RHODES	ENG	1	33.51	31.01	54
50	WALTERS	AUS	3	33.02	35.38	44
51	J DARLING	AUS	1	32.99	30.79	55
52	BELL	ENG	5	32.85	35.41	43
53	KNOTT	ENG	3/4	32.20	32.98	51
54	WOOLLEY	ENG	2	32.13	33.28	50
55	BOTHAM	ENG	4	32.00	29.35	59
56	HENDREN	ENG	2	31.64	39.55	34
57	GOOCH	ENG	4	31.07	33.31	49
58	A STEWART	ENG	4	29.84	30.67	57
59	R MARSH	AUS	3/4	28.33	27.21	60
60	ATHERTON	ENG	4	27.62	29.68	58
61	S GREGORY	AUS	1	27.48	25.80	61

BOWLERS IN ORDER OF WKTS TAKEN

			ERA	M	W	RAW AV	RAW RK	ADJ AV	ADJ RK
1	WARNE	AUS	4/5	36	195	23.25	15	21.15	3
2	LILLEE	AUS	3/4	29	167	21.00	9	22.41	5
3	MCGRATH	AUS	4/5	30	157	20.92	8	20.39	2
4	BOTHAM	ENG	4	36	148	27.65	31	28.37	34
5	TRUMBLE	AUS	1	31	141	20.88	7	25.59	18
6	WILLIS	ENG	3/4	35	128	26.14	26	28.96	38
7	S BROAD	ENG	5	32	118	29.36	33	27.16	30
8	NOBLE	AUS	1	39	115	24.86	20	28.33	33
9	LINDWALL	AUS	3	29	114	22.44	14	24.02	10
10	RHODES	ENG	1	41	109	24.00	17	27.88	32
11	S BARNES	ENG	1	20	106	21.58	12	24.86	15
12	GRIMMETT	AUS	2	22	106	32.44	40	26.99	28
13	UNDERWOOD	ENG	3/4	29	105	26.38	28	26.39	23
14	BEDSER	ENG	3	21	104	27.49	30	26.82	26
15	ANDERSON	ENG	5	32	104	34.57	42	30.55	40
16	GIFFEN	AUS	1	31	103	27.09	29	33.24	43
17	O'REILLY	AUS	2	19	102	25.36	23	23.24	7
18	TURNER	AUS	1	17	101	16.53	2	28.65	37
19	PEEL	ENG	1	20	101	16.98	3	25.14	17
20	ALDERMAN	AUS	4	17	100	21.17	10	22.15	4
21	THOMSON	AUS	3/4	21	100	24.18	18	24.09	11
22	BRIGGS	ENG	1	31	97	20.55	6	25.72	20
23	LAWSON	AUS	4	21	97	28.48	32	24.56	14
24	MCKENZIE	AUS	3	25	96	31.34	38	28.57	36
25	SPOFFORTH	AUS	1	18	94	18.41	5	28.49	35
26	RICHARDSON	ENG	1	14	88	25.22	21	26.64	25
27	MILLER	AUS	3	29	87	22.40	13	24.20	12
28	M JOHNSON	AUS	5	19	87	25.82	25	23.89	9
29	MAILEY	AUS	2	18	86	34.12	41	27.39	31
30	LYON	AUS	5	23	85	30.53	36	29.60	39

			ERA	M	W	RAW AV	RAW RK	ADJ AV	ADJ RK
31	DAVIDSON	AUS	3	25	84	23.76	16	24.97	16
32	MCDERMOTT	AUS	4	17	84	26.31	27	23.04	6
33	SNOW	ENG	3	20	83	25.61	24	24.40	13
34	TATE	ENG	2	20	83	30.60	37	23.74	8
35	BENAUD	AUS	3	27	83	31.81	39	32.98	42
36	SIDDLE	AUS	5	24	80	29.81	34	26.84	27
37	LAKER	ENG	3	15	79	18.27	4	19.79	1
38	TRUEMAN	ENG	3	19	79	25.30	22	26.52	24
39	EMBUREY	ENG	4	25	78	34.59	43	31.85	41
40	PALMER	AUS	1	17	78	21.51	11	27.10	29
41	LOHMANN	ENG	1	15	77	13.01	1	25.68	19
42	JOHNSTON	AUS	3	17	75	24.24	19	25.94	21
43	M HUGHES	AUS	4	20	75	30.25	35	26.25	22

BOWLERS RAW RANKINGS

		🏴	ERA	RAW AV	ADJ AV	ADJ RK
1	LOHMANN	ENG	1	13.01	25.68	19
2	TURNER	AUS	1	16.53	28.65	37
3	PEEL	ENG	1	16.98	25.14	17
4	LAKER	ENG	3	18.27	19.79	1
5	SPOFFORTH	AUS	1	18.41	28.49	35
6	BRIGGS	ENG	1	20.55	25.72	20
7	TRUMBLE	AUS	1	20.88	25.59	18
8	MCGRATH	AUS	4/5	20.92	20.39	2
9	LILLEE	AUS	3/4	21.00	22.41	5
10	ALDERMAN	AUS	4	21.17	22.15	4
11	PALMER	AUS	1	21.51	27.10	29
12	S BARNES	ENG	1	21.58	24.86	15
13	MILLER	AUS	3	22.40	24.20	12
14	LINDWALL	AUS	3	22.44	24.02	10
15	WARNE	AUS	4/5	23.25	21.15	3
16	DAVIDSON	AUS	3	23.76	24.97	16
17	RHODES	ENG	1	24.00	27.88	32
18	THOMSON	AUS	3/4	24.18	24.09	11
19	JOHNSTON	AUS	3	24.24	25.94	21
20	NOBLE	AUS	1	24.86	28.33	33
21	RICHARDSON	ENG	1	25.22	26.64	25
22	TRUEMAN	ENG	3	25.30	26.52	24
23	O'REILLY	AUS	2	25.36	23.24	7
24	SNOW	ENG	3	25.61	24.40	13
25	M JOHNSON	AUS	5	25.82	23.89	9
26	WILLIS	ENG	3/4	26.14	28.96	38
27	MCDERMOTT	AUS	4	26.31	23.04	6
28	UNDERWOOD	ENG	3/4	26.38	26.39	23
29	GIFFEN	AUS	1	27.09	33.24	43
30	BEDSER	ENG	3	27.49	26.82	26

		ERA	RAW AV	ADJ AV	ADJ RK
31	BOTHAM	ENG	4	27.65	28.37	34
32	LAWSON	AUS	4	28.48	24.56	14
33	S BROAD	ENG	5	29.36	27.16	30
34	SIDDLE	AUS	5	29.81	26.84	27
35	M HUGHES	AUS	4	30.25	26.25	22
36	LYON	AUS	5	30.53	29.60	39
37	TATE	ENG	2	30.60	23.74	8
38	MCKENZIE	AUS	3	31.34	28.57	36
39	BENAUD	AUS	3	31.81	32.98	42
40	GRIMMETT	AUS	2	32.44	26.99	28
41	MAILEY	AUS	2	34.12	27.39	31
42	ANDERSON	ENG	5	34.57	30.55	40
43	EMBUREY	ENG	4	34.59	31.85	41

BOWLERS ADJUSTED RANKINGS

		⚑	ERA	ADJ AV	RAW AV	RAW RK
1	LAKER	ENG	3	19.79	18.27	4
2	MCGRATH	AUS	4/5	20.39	20.92	8
3	WARNE	AUS	4/5	21.15	23.25	15
4	ALDERMAN	AUS	4	22.15	21.17	10
5	LILLEE	AUS	3/4	22.41	21.00	9
6	MCDERMOTT	AUS	4	23.04	26.31	27
7	O'REILLY	AUS	2	23.24	25.36	23
8	TATE	ENG	2	23.74	30.60	37
9	M JOHNSON	AUS	5	23.89	25.82	25
10	LINDWALL	AUS	3	24.02	22.44	14
11	THOMSON	AUS	3/4	24.09	24.18	18
12	MILLER	AUS	3	24.20	22.40	13
13	SNOW	ENG	3	24.40	25.61	24
14	LAWSON	AUS	4	24.56	28.48	32
15	S BARNES	ENG	1	24.86	21.58	12
16	DAVIDSON	AUS	3	24.97	23.76	16
17	PEEL	ENG	1	25.14	16.98	3
18	TRUMBLE	AUS	1	25.59	20.88	7
19	LOHMANN	ENG	1	25.68	13.01	1
20	BRIGGS	ENG	1	25.72	20.55	6
21	JOHNSTON	AUS	3	25.94	24.24	19
22	M HUGHES	AUS	4	26.25	30.25	35
23	UNDERWOOD	ENG	3/4	26.39	26.38	28
24	TRUEMAN	ENG	3	26.52	25.30	22
25	RICHARDSON	ENG	1	26.64	25.22	21
26	BEDSER	ENG	3	26.82	27.49	30
27	SIDDLE	AUS	5	26.84	29.81	34
28	GRIMMETT	AUS	2	26.99	32.44	40
29	PALMER	AUS	1	27.10	21.51	11
30	S BROAD	ENG	5	27.16	29.36	33

			ERA	ADJ AV	RAW AV	RAW RK
31	MAILEY	AUS	2	27.39	34.12	41
32	RHODES	ENG	1	27.88	24.00	17
33	NOBLE	AUS	1	28.33	24.86	20
34	BOTHAM	ENG	4	28.37	27.65	31
35	SPOFFORTH	AUS	1	28.49	18.41	5
36	MCKENZIE	AUS	3	28.57	31.34	38
37	TURNER	AUS	1	28.65	16.53	2
38	WILLIS	ENG	3/4	28.96	26.14	26
39	LYON	AUS	5	29.60	30.53	36
40	ANDERSON	ENG	5	30.55	34.57	42
41	EMBUREY	ENG	4	31.85	34.59	43
42	BENAUD	AUS	3	32.98	31.81	39
43	GIFFEN	AUS	1	33.24	27.09	29

ENGLAND CAPTAINS

(in chronological order of first match as captain)

		SPAN	MATCHES	WON	LOST	DRAWN	%
1	LILLYWHITE	1877	2	1	1	0	50
2	HARRIS	1879-84	4	2	1	1	63
3	SHAW	1881-82	4	0	2	2	25
4	HORNBY	1882-84	2	0	1	1	25
5	BLIGH	1882-83	4	2	2	0	50
6	SHREWSBURY	1884-87	7	5	2	0	71
7	STEEL	1886-88	4	3	1	0	75
8	READ	1888	1	1	0	0	100
9	GRACE	1888-99	13	8	3	2	69
10	STODDART	1893-98	8	3	4	1	44
11	MACLAREN	1897-09	22	4	11	7	34
12	P WARNER	1903-04	5	3	2	0	60
13	JACKSON	1905	5	2	0	3	70
14	FANE	1907-08	3	1	2	0	33
15	A JONES	1908	2	0	2	0	0
16	DOUGLAS	1911-21	12	4	8	0	33
17	FRY	1912	3	1	0	2	67
18	TENNYSON	1921	3	0	1	2	33
19	GILLIGAN	1924-25	5	1	4	0	20
20	CARR	1926	4	0	0	4	50
21	CHAPMAN	1926-30	9	6	1	2	78
22	WHITE	1929	1	0	1	0	0
23	WYATT	1930-34	5	1	2	2	40
24	JARDINE	1932-33	5	4	1	0	80
25	WALTERS	1934	1	0	1	0	0
26	ALLEN	1936-37	5	2	3	0	40
27	HAMMOND	1938-47	8	1	3	4	38
28	YARDLEY	1947-48	6	0	5	1	8
29	BROWN	1950-51	5	1	4	0	20

		SPAN	MATCHES	WON	LOST	DRAWN	%
30	HUTTON	1953-55	10	4	1	5	65
31	MAY	1956-61	13	3	6	4	38
32	COWDREY	1961-68	6	1	2	3	42
33	DEXTER	1962-64	10	1	2	7	45
34	M SMITH	1965-66	5	1	1	3	50
35	GRAVENEY	1968	1	0	0	1	50
36	ILLINGWORTH	1970-72	11	4	2	5	59
37	DENNESS	1974-75	6	1	4	1	25
38	J EDRICH	1975	1	0	1	0	0
39	GREIG	1975-77	4	0	1	3	38
40	BREARLEY	1977-81	18	11	4	3	69
41	BOTHAM	1980-81	3	0	1	2	33
42	WILLIS	1982-83	5	1	2	2	40
43	GOWER	1985-89	12	3	5	4	42
44	GATTING	1986-88	6	2	1	3	58
45	LAMB	1990	1	0	1	0	0
46	GOOCH	1990-93	8	0	5	3	19
47	ATHERTON	1993-01	15	4	9	2	33
48	A STEWART	1998-99	5	1	3	1	30
49	HUSSAIN	2001-03	8	2	6	0	25
50	VAUGHAN	2005	5	2	1	2	60
51	FLINTOFF	2006-07	5	0	5	0	0
52	STRAUSS	2009-11	10	5	2	3	65
53	COOK	2013-15	15	6	7	2	47
54	ROOT	2017-	10	2	6	2	30
			351	110	146	95	44.9%

ENGLAND CAPTAINS

(in order of success percentage)

		SPAN	MATCHES	WON	LOST	DRAWN	%
1	READ	1888	1	1	0	0	100
2	JARDINE	1932-33	5	4	1	0	80
3	CHAPMAN	1926-30	9	6	1	2	78
4	STEEL	1886-88	4	3	1	0	75
5	SHREWSBURY	1884-87	7	5	2	0	71
6	JACKSON	1905	5	2	0	3	70
7	GRACE	1888-99	13	8	3	2	69
8	BREARLEY	1977-81	18	11	4	3	69
9	FRY	1912	3	1	0	2	67
10	HUTTON	1953-55	10	4	1	5	65
11	STRAUSS	2009-11	10	5	2	3	65
12	HARRIS	1879-84	4	2	1	1	63
13	P WARNER	1903-04	5	3	2	0	60
14	VAUGHAN	2005	5	2	1	2	60
15	ILLINGWORTH	1970-72	11	4	2	5	59
16	GATTING	1986-88	6	2	1	3	58
17	LILLYWHITE	1877	2	1	1	0	50
18	BLIGH	1882-83	4	2	2	0	50
19	CARR	1926	4	0	0	4	50
20	M SMITH	1965-66	5	1	1	3	50
21	GRAVENEY	1968	1	0	0	1	50
22	COOK	2013-15	15	6	7	2	47
23	DEXTER	1962-64	10	1	2	7	45
24	STODDART	1893-98	8	3	4	1	44
25	COWDREY	1961-68	6	1	2	3	42
26	GOWER	1985-89	12	3	5	4	42
27	WYATT	1930-34	5	1	2	2	40
28	ALLEN	1936-37	5	2	3	0	40
29	WILLIS	1982-83	5	1	2	2	40

		SPAN	MATCHES	WON	LOST	DRAWN	%
30	HAMMOND	1938-47	8	1	3	4	38
31	MAY	1956-61	13	3	6	4	38
32	GREIG	1975-77	4	0	1	3	38
33	MACLAREN	1897-09	22	4	11	7	34
34	FANE	1907-08	3	1	2	0	33
35	DOUGLAS	1911-21	12	4	8	0	33
36	TENNYSON	1921	3	0	1	2	33
37	BOTHAM	1980-81	3	0	1	2	33
38	ATHERTON	1993-01	15	4	9	2	33
39	A STEWART	1998-99	5	1	3	1	30
40	ROOT	2017-	10	2	6	2	30
41	SHAW	1881-82	4	0	2	2	25
42	HORNBY	1882-84	2	0	1	1	25
43	DENNESS	1974-75	6	1	4	1	25
44	HUSSAIN	2001-03	8	2	6	0	25
45	GILLIGAN	1924-25	5	1	4	0	20
46	BROWN	1950-51	5	1	4	0	20
47	GOOCH	1990-93	8	0	5	3	19
48	YARDLEY	1947-48	6	0	5	1	8
49	A JONES	1908	2	0	2	0	0
50	WHITE	1929	1	0	1	0	0
51	WALTERS	1934	1	0	1	0	0
52	J EDRICH	1975	1	0	1	0	0
53	LAMB	1990	1	0	1	0	0
54	FLINTOFF	2006-07	5	0	5	0	0
			351	110	146	95	44.9%

AUSTRALIAN CAPTAINS

(in chronological order of first match as captain)

		SPAN	MATCHES	WON	LOST	DRAWN	%
1	D GREGORY	1877-79	3	2	1	0	67
2	MURDOCH	1880-90	16	5	7	4	44
3	HORAN	1885	2	0	2	0	0
4	MASSIE	1885	1	1	0	0	100
5	BLACKHAM	1885-94	8	3	3	2	50
6	SCOTT	1886	3	0	3	0	0
7	MCDONNELL	1887-88	6	1	5	0	17
8	GIFFEN	1894-95	4	2	2	0	50
9	TROTT	1896-98	8	5	3	0	63
10	J DARLING	1899-05	18	5	4	9	53
11	TRUMBLE	1902	2	2	0	0	100
12	NOBLE	1903-09	15	8	5	2	60
13	C HILL	1911-12	5	1	4	0	20
14	S GREGORY	1912	3	0	1	2	33
15	ARMSTRONG	1920-21	10	8	0	2	90
16	COLLINS	1924-26	8	4	2	2	63
17	BARDSLEY	1926	2	0	0	2	50
18	RYDER	1928-29	5	1	4	0	20
19	WOODFULL	1930-34	15	5	6	4	47
20	BRADMAN	1936-48	19	11	3	5	71
21	HASSETT	1950-53	10	4	2	4	60
22	I JOHNSON	1954-56	9	2	4	3	39
23	MORRIS	1954	1	0	1	0	0
24	BENAUD	1958-63	14	6	2	6	64
25	HARVEY	1961	1	1	0	0	100
26	SIMPSON	1964-66	8	2	0	6	63
27	BOOTH	1965-66	2	0	1	1	25
28	LAWRY	1968-71	9	1	2	6	44
29	JARMAN	1968	1	0	0	1	50

		SPAN	MATCHES	WON	LOST	DRAWN	%
30	I CHAPPELL	1971-75	16	7	4	5	59
31	G CHAPPELL	1977-83	15	6	4	5	57
32	YALLOP	1978-79	6	1	5	0	17
33	K HUGHES	1981	6	1	3	2	33
34	BORDER	1985-93	29	13	6	10	62
35	M TAYLOR	1994-99	16	9	4	3	66
36	S WAUGH	2001-03	9	8	1	0	89
37	GILCHRIST	2001	1	0	1	0	0
38	PONTING	2005-10	19	8	6	5	55
39	CLARKE	2011-15	16	7	7	2	50
40	S SMITH	2017-18	5	4	0	1	90
41	PAINE	2019-	5	2	2	1	50
			351	146	110	95	55.1%

AUSTRALIAN CAPTAINS

(in order of success percentage)

		SPAN	MATCHES	WON	LOST	DRAWN	%
1	MASSIE	1885	1	1	0	0	100
2	TRUMBLE	1902	2	2	0	0	100
3	HARVEY	1961	1	1	0	0	100
4	ARMSTRONG	1920-21	10	8	0	2	90
5	S SMITH	2017-	5	4	0	1	90
6	S WAUGH	2001-03	9	8	1	0	89
7	BRADMAN	1936-48	19	11	3	5	71
8	D GREGORY	1877-79	3	2	1	0	67
9	M TAYLOR	1994-99	16	9	4	3	66
10	BENAUD	1958-63	14	6	2	6	64
11	TROTT	1896-98	8	5	3	0	63
12	COLLINS	1924-26	8	4	2	2	63
13	SIMPSON	1964-66	8	2	0	6	63
14	BORDER	1985-93	29	13	6	10	62
15	NOBLE	1903-09	15	8	5	2	60
16	HASSETT	1950-53	10	4	2	4	60
17	I CHAPPELL	1971-75	16	7	4	5	59
18	G CHAPPELL	1977-83	15	6	4	5	57
19	PONTING	2005-10	19	8	6	5	55
20	J DARLING	1899-05	18	5	4	9	53
21	CLARKE	2011-15	16	7	7	2	50
22	BLACKHAM	1885-94	8	3	3	2	50
23	GIFFEN	1894-95	4	2	2	0	50
24	BARDSLEY	1926	2	0	0	2	50
25	JARMAN	1968	1	0	0	1	50
26	PAINE	2019-	5	2	2	1	50
27	WOODFULL	1930-34	15	5	6	4	47
28	MURDOCH	1880-90	16	5	7	4	44
29	LAWRY	1968-71	9	1	2	6	44

		SPAN	MATCHES	WON	LOST	DRAWN	%
30	I JOHNSON	1954-56	9	2	4	3	39
31	S GREGORY	1912	3	0	1	2	33
32	M HUGHES	1981	6	1	3	2	33
33	BOOTH	1965-66	2	0	1	1	25
34	C HILL	1911-12	5	1	4	0	20
35	RYDER	1928-29	5	1	4	0	20
36	MCDONNELL	1887-88	6	1	5	0	17
37	YALLOP	1978-79	6	1	5	0	17
38	HORAN	1885	2	0	2	0	0
39	SCOTT	1886	3	0	3	0	0
40	MORRIS	1954	1	0	1	0	0
41	GILCHRIST	2001	1	0	1	0	0
			351	146	110	95	55.1%

DAVID COOKE

WAS GRACE
BETTER THAN
BRADMAN?

A NEW WAY TO RANK ASHES CRICKETERS